THE ENCHANTED

Frontispiece: Six-foot menhir from Kallerup, Secland, which dates from AD 700-800. The runic inscription reads 'Hornture's Store, Swithing [=Swithe's son]' (*from Stephens, 1884*).

THE ENCHANTED ALPHABET

A Guide to Authentic Rune Magic and Divination

Dr James M. Peterson

Illustrations by Dr Marjorie Whitsitt

THE AQUARIAN PRESS

To Marjorie

First published 1988

© James M. Peterson 1988

British Library Cataloguing in Publication Data

Peterson, James M.
The enchanted alphabet: a guide to
authentic rune magic and divination
1. Runes. Occult aspects
I. Title
133.3'3

ISBN 0-85030-765-1

The Aquarian Press is part of the Thorsons Publishing Group, Wellingborough, Northamptonshire, NN8 2RQ, England

Printed in Great Britain by by Woolnough Bookbinding
Limited, Irthlingborough, Northamptonshire
Typeset by MJL Limited, Hitchin, Hertfordshire

1 3 5 7 9 10 8 6 4 2

CONTENTS

INTRODUCTION

Beech runes are there,
  birth runes are there,
And all the runes of ale,
  and the magic runes of might.
Who knows them rightly
  and reads them true
Has them himself to help;
  and ever they aid
Until the gods are dead.
                              —Havamal

Nearly two thousand years ago the Germanic peoples of northern Europe created a set of letters which they called the 'runes', from their word for 'secret'. These letters were chiselled into granite monuments and gravestones to commemorate famous men and great deeds, and were carved or branded into wood to carry commonplace messages. But from the very first they were much more than an ordinary alphabet, for each letter had a mystical meaning and the entire set of twenty-four characters was thought to have magical power. The runes were an indispensable part of northern European sorcery: they were used for foretelling the future, for creating healing magic, and for working deadly curses.

There has been a recent resurgence of interest in the use of the runes for working magical rites and for casting fortunes. This book teaches theories and methods for doing both.

In order to use the runes in their occult aspects, one needs to know two things: what the symbolic values or meanings of the runes are, and how these meanings are activated in practical magical and divinatory applications. Unfortunately, a great deal of information about just how the runes were used, and their precise meanings, has become obscured in the centuries since this old Germanic alphabet last saw widespread common use.

The problem of interpretation is further complicated by the fact that the runes changed across time and from one place to another as the various languages branched out in their evolution from their old Germanic base. Two distinct runic traditions emerged in the years after about AD 600 In England and Frisia, rune-masters set about adding characters as they needed them for new sounds so that the letters in their system grew in number from the original twenty-four to thirty-one. During the same period, reformers among the Norsemen took the opposite tack. They *reduced* the number of runes in their system by eight, simplified some of the letter shapes, and changed some of the phonetic values and the esoteric meanings. They ended up with a drastically modified alphabet of only sixteen characters by about AD 800.

There is an Anglo-Saxon poem which gives one version of the meanings of the runes. The first stanza looks like this in the original:

> Feoh byþ frofur
>   fira gewhylcum;
> sceal Ðeah manna gehwylc
>   miclun hyt daelan
> gif he wile for drihtne
>   domes hleotan

It means 'Feoh, (Fehu: property, wealth) is a comfort to everyone; yet one must give it away in order to gain merit in the eyes of God.'

There is still an extant English folk tradition of using the runes for fortune-telling based upon this rune poem, but the poem seems to have been subjected to the depredations of time as well as to considerable incursions of Christian influence by the time it was written down in the earliest form which has survived; the letter meanings are both obscured and considerably diluted from the vibrancy of the original pagan meanings and usages. The poem gives 'thorn' in place of the original *Thurs*, 'giant'; 'sedge-grass' is substituted for 'elk' (which is the North American 'moose'), etc. And not a great deal seems to remain in the folk consciousness about the use of the old letters for sorcery.

I have sought to trace the runic letters and the practices connected with them back as far as possible toward their original forms and values, and to reconstruct, in so far as is possible, the states of mind with which the early rune-masters approached their art. In general, one does this sort of tracing in three ways. First, there is sometimes direct evidence from the early periods. For example, the archaeological evidence does not leave us in much doubt about the physical shape of the early runes, and Roman writers such as Cornelius Tacitus wrote at considerable length about the quaint customs and beliefs of their potential and traditional enemies, the Germanic tribes.

Second, antiquarians from various fields have been reasonably successful in reconstructing the Teutonic tongue and religion as they must have been in the days when the runes were being created. The importance of this work can hardly be overstated, for the language gave the names of the runes, and the religion supplied much of the associated symbolism.

And third, cross-correspondences in the evidence from various later sources may allow one to make a reasonable guess at the original meaning of a rune. For this purpose I have deliberately favoured the Scandinavian archaelogical data and Icelandic/Old Norse literature: the poetic and prose Eddas, the historic sagas, and the skaldic poems, because these sources stand either within or closer to the pagan tradition, but certain Old English writings and runic inscriptions are sometimes useful for comparative purposes. As an example of how a meaning may be established through comparisons across sources, see my discussion of the PER—ÐRA/PERU rune (No. 14).

In conjunction with these methods, the student can sometimes develop insights about the meaning of the runes through Jungian psychology. Where only the literal meaning of a rune is known, one can sometimes get a hint of a the broader meaning by treating the known forms as manifestations of an archetype, and then seeking the meanings of that archetype in other symbologies where they may be more fully elaborated. The French scholar Georges

Dumezil has written extensively on the relationships among the gods and myths of the various Indo-European peoples, showing us how connections can be traced between the pantheons of peoples as diverse as the Greeks and Romans, the Hindus and the Germanic tribes.

There is a fourth method which I sometimes employed, but always with the utmost caution: namely, the process of collecting empirical data from divination. By working with the runes, one eventually gets a feel for their individual characters and meanings, especially as one compares predictive readings with subsequent events.

I recall vividly the first time I carved out a set of divinatory rune pieces from oak and consecrated them. As soon as I had finished the coin sacrifice ritual and prayer, I asked for a sign that the sacrifice had been accepted and reached into my rune bag. For all the world it felt to me as if one of the pieces had come alive to wriggle out from among its fellows and into my fingers. I pulled this rune from the bag and examined it. It was URUS, the rune which my early studies told me stood for strength. The compelling nature of this experience made me look into the meaning of the rune more deeply, and I soon discovered that URUS stands for magical potency, or *megin*, as well as for physical strength: the URUS rune was telling me that the hallowing rite had 'taken,' and the rune set had acquired the power which I had sought for it. In the process, this reading also forced me to enrich my understanding of the symbolism and the underlying theory of rune magic.

As with the URUS reading, in any case where my own rune work has apparently brought forward, amplified, or clarified a rune meaning, I have always sought to confirm this use from another source. If such confirmation cannot be found, I have invariably viewed my finding as tentative, and have withheld it. Too much unwarranted (and sometimes demonstrably incorrect) speculation about the meanings of the runes has already seen print.

For the most part, I have spared the reader the details of the research which I undertook in order to establish the meanings of the characters — especially in those instances where my independent work confirmed popularly available sources such as the two articles from *Fate* Magazine listed in the bibliography.

However, where my results are substantially different from

other published interpretations I reported the lines of evidence
and interpretation which led me to my heresies. The serious
inquirer will find these arguments appended to the discussion of the various runes which present difficulties.

Just as every human being exists in the context of one or
another specific culture, so does every symbolic system. One
cannot have much success with the *I Ching* without learning to slip (at least somewhat) into a classical Chinese
philosophical perspective, and students of the Kabbalah must
learn the world-view of medieval Judaism. The study of the
runes places no less of a demand on the student that she learn
something about the ways in which the ancient Germanic
tribes perceived the world. I have tried in these pages to pro-
vide an introduction to that frame of mind, to give the reader
a glimpse of the world as the northern Europeans of fifteen
centuries ago saw it. In seeking this end, I have made free
use of insights offered by various social sciences. I borrowed
and learned from archaeology and cultural anthropology,
from Jungian theory, from William James's writings on the
laws of mind, and from the developmental psychology of Jean
Piaget.

As it happens, I came to the study of the old nordic belief
system with a background in academic psychology and some
knowledge, both personal and professional, of Ojibwa Indian
culture. I was born a few miles from an Ojibwa reservation
in northern Wisconsin and have had Indian people as friends
all my life. I studied certain aspects of Indian culture and personality in my doctoral research and after. I was thus in a
position to note that there are many points of commonality
between the world-views of the Indians and of the old northern Europeans, as evidenced in the practice of shamanism,
a belief in magic, certain beliefs about the spirit-world and
the relationship of man to his physical and human environ-
ment, and so on. The reader will be able to see for himself
some of the ways in which these aspects of my personal history have coloured my understanding of Germanic paganism.

In her admirable book *Gods and Myths of Northern
Europe*, H.R. Ellis Davidson has these words of caution,
which I echo and endorse, for anyone who wishes to begin
the voyage of discovery into the realms of the old religion:

We must be prepared for the simple folk beliefs of the less sophisti-
cated to be found alongside complex symbolism. The important thing

is not to allow the crudity of the folk beliefs to blind us to the depth and importance of the symbolism. Crude and childish ideas about the heathen gods will certainly be found in the myths, either because these satisfied ignorant folk, or because the use of symbols has been misunderstood by the recorder. But it does not follow that all who worshipped these gods were crude and childish in their outlook. Indeed, the contention put forward in this book is that this was very far from the case.[1]

The runes were invented primarily as tools of sorcery and divination, and for communication with the unseen universe. Their symbolism deals with those matters which the ancient Teutonic pagans thought most important in their relationship with their gods and with the powers which they conceived to be at large in their world. As a result, the runes are the most direct route available into the ways of thought and the occult practices of these long-dead people; but the rewards for studying the runes are not merely in their practical applications, for the person who follows this trail will accomplish two other purposes of even greater significance. She will have become familiar with a world-view which is not strained to breaking by the growing evidence that paranormal events exists; and second, she will have acquired a perspective which provides common philosophical ground with that majority of humanity who live still today within cultures and world-views which accept magic as a given aspect of the universe.

At times one feels overwhelmed by the failings of the old pagans; sickened by their pirate raids and slave trade and endless blood feuds, disgusted by their taste for animal and even human sacrifices. But we live in a world where weapons sufficient to destroy life on earth already exist in plenty, and yet people race to build more. We live in times when farmers are being devastated at an increasing rate, drowning in the fruits of their own productivity, and yet many others on earth are dying of starvation. Can we seriously expect that history will see us as a more civilized race?

A NOTE ON SPELLING

The old Germanic languages differed considerably in pronunciation from modern English. For the most part the reader need not be concerned with these phonetic technicalities. I have, however, used two special characters in spelling the rune

The helmeted head of a warrior curved from Elk antler and found in Sigtuna, Sweden (*from the National Antiquities Museum, Stockholm, Sweden*).

names and other words in the old languages. These characters stand for sounds which are not used in English. Đ represents a consonant midway between the voiced 'th' in 'this' and the 'd' sound heard in 'dog'. Ƶ is also a sound which stands midway between two consonants, in this case a trilled 'r' and a 'z' sound.

PART ONE:
THE BACKGROUND OF THE RUNES

1. THE HISTORICAL CONTEXT

The archaeological evidence tells us that the runic system of writing was invented no later than the second century AD, hundreds of years before the Viking era began. Even so, many people call them the 'Viking runes', for about the same reason so many Scandinavians think of themselves as descended from those old sea rovers (as opposed, say, to landlocked peasants): that is, pure romanticism. In fact, the versions of the runes which were in use in Scandinavia and Iceland during Viking times were late, localized variations on the original forms with which this book is mostly concerned.

Our word 'alphabet' comes from 'alpha' and 'beta', the Greek words for the first two letters, A and B. In a similar way, the runes are sometimes known as the 'Futhark' from the pronunciation of the first six characters in their conventional order, ᚠᚢᚦᚨᚱᚲ. The runic ᚦ ('Th') is a single letter equivalent to the Old English Thorn.

From their point of origin, quite likely on Jutland, the Danish peninsula, the runes spread throughout the Germanic peoples. These Germanic tribes were the ancestors of the modern Scandinavians, Germans, Dutch, Frisians, and English. In their early forms, all of these languages continued to be written in runes as they evolved away from each other.

We know that the Germanic peoples had, about two millenia before the time of Christ, given up a hunting and gathering existence to be farmers. In those days as now, religions evolved to

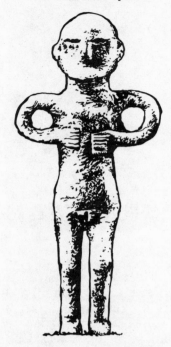

Figure 1: Bronze Age Fertility Goddess from the bog at Viksø.

fit new circumstances. In this case, the Germanic tribes adopted some new gods and goddesses, whom they called the Vanir, into their pantheon. The older gods — the Aesir — were gods fit for worship by nomadic warriors. Among them were Wotan (Odin), Frigg, TiwaZ (later called Tyr), Thor, Ullr, Heimdall, Loki, Balder, and others.

The Vanir, however, were gods with more to offer a farming people who sought supernatural aid in such matters as increasing the fruitfulness of their fields and of their domestic animals. Tacitus writes in AD 98 of a fertility rite among several tribes of the Germans who were then living on the Danish peninsula:

> These tribes. . . worship in common Nerthus, or Mother Earth, and conceive her as intervening in human affairs, and riding in procession through the cities of men. In an island of the ocean is a holy grove, and in it a consecrated chariot (*vehiculum*) covered with a robe: A single priest is permitted to touch it: he feels the presence of the goddess in her shrine, and follows with deep reverence as she rides away drawn by cows: then come days of rejoicing, and all places keep holiday, as many as she thinks

worthy to receive and entertain her. They make no war, take no arms: every weapon is put away; peace and quiet are then, and then alone, known and loved, until the same priest returns the goddess to her sacred precinct, when she has had her fill of the society of mortals. After this the chariot and the robe, and if you are willing to credit it, the deity in person, are washed in a sequestered lake: slaves are the ministrants and are straightaway swallowed by the same lake: hence a mysterious terror and an ignorance full of piety as to what that may be which men only behold to die.[2]

The Nerthus rite underwent some changes in the succeeding centuries. The chariot (Figure 1) was later drawn by horses rather than cattle. By a process not fully understood by modern scholars the Goddess Nerthus seems to have evolved into the God Njörd. The chariot in later times seems to have carried a sundisc rather than the Goddess (Figure 2), and Nerthus/Njörd's children, Freyr and Freya, took over some of the ceremonial responsibilities.

The importance of this rite is considerable for our present quest to understand the runes since it seems to have played a large role in the selection of the symbols which underly the Futhark. Consider, for example, the number of runes which derive their imagery from the ceremony: We have the chariot (RAIÐU) represented, along with the cattle (FEHU) (or horses, EHWAZ) that pulled it. INGWAZ represents the gods worshipped in the ceremony; the sun (SOWELU) which in some versions of the rite rode the chariot with the gods is among the runes, along with

Figure 2: Nerthus rite chariot, used to transport an image of the fertility goddess. This wagon was found in the moors of Deibjerg in West Jutland and restored.

the bountiful year (JARA) for which the farmers made sacrifice
(GEBU), hoping the gods would cause their harvests and children to increase to the people might escape want (NAUÐIZ)
which could result from hail (HAGALAZ) or the other agricultural calamities it symbolized, and so on.

Chariots, sun-discs, horse and cattle sculptures, and other
paraphernalia associated with the rite have been dug up from
gravesites, bogs, and marshes throughout the Germanic world,
from middle Europe to Iceland. These finds have been dated
from pre-Christian times to sometime after the first millenium.
This basic fertility rite, though it varied somewhat across space
and time, remained the most important religio-magical event
in the lives of the pagan Germanic tribesmen for at least two
millennia, and perhaps nearer three. It is impossible to appre-
hend the true nature of the runic symbols without some
understanding of the cultural milieu from which they sprang.

SHAMANS

The Germanic tribes had among them various classes of holy
persons, sorcerers, and foretellers of the future. The ones with
the greatest power—especially in the early days of the culture—
were those who had sought out contact with the spirit world
through a vision quest.

The most famous description of a vision quest in the Germanic
tradition occurs in the Havamal (Stanzas 139-42, here slightly
modified from Bellows' translation) in which Odin describes
how he got wisdom, the gift of poetry, and knowledge of the runes
themselves:

> I know that I hung
>   on that wind-tossed tree,
>   Swung there for nine full nights;
> With my spear I was wounded,
>   and offered I was
>   To Odin, myself to myself,
> On the tree that none
>   may ever know
>   What root beneath it runs.
>
> None made me happy
>   with loaf or horn,
>   And there below I looked;
> I took up the runes,
>   shrieking I took them,
>   And forthwith back I fell.

Nine mighty songs
  I got from the son
Of Bolthorn, Bestla's father;
And a drink I got
  of the goodly mead
Poured out from Othrörir.

Then I began to thrive,
  and wisdom to get,
I grew and well I was;
Each word led me
  on to another word,
Each deed to another deed.[3]

Bizarre as these lines may sound to the casual reader of today, the poem describes what was undoubtedly a real custom in the pagan Germanic culture. And still today we can find societies, such as certain remote Siberian groups, in which the vision quest is practised.

Modern anthropologists use the Siberian word 'shaman' to describe individuals who seek direct contact with the spirit world through a vision quest or various other means such as meditation or drugs. Those who go through the experience typically acquire the power to command supernatural forces, bewitch or heal others, find lost things, identify wrongdoers, communicate with the dead, and foretell the future.

The Ojibwa Indians of the Lake Superior region of North

Figure 3: 'And a drink I got of the goodly mead Poured out from Othrorir. Odin on his eight-legged horse Sleipmer (a portion of the eighth-century Jutland stone at Olskog, Tjangvide, Sweden).

America have raised the practice of the vision quest to a high art. In most cultures (including the early Germanic peoples) only a few exceptional visionaries ever undertake the quest, and they usually become sorcerers and spiritual leaders as a result. Among the Ojibwa, however, the vision quest was the principal male rite of passage into adulthood; one could not become a man until he experienced a 'life-dream' in which he would be visited by a guardian spirit who would adopt and care for him through all the years of his life. Until the young Indian obtained his vision he would be a trial and burden to his family and clan. In consequence, *every young male* was expected to go through the vision quest—not merely to attempt to receive a supernatural visitation but to succeed in obtaining it.

Women went through a briefer period of isolation and fasting at the time of their first menstrual flow. Although they were not expected and certainly not encouraged to seek contact with 'spirit-helpers', they sometimes had visions and acquired supernatural guardians anyway.

Much has been written about the Ojibwa vision quest custom, but few reports are better than one by the German traveller and adventurer Johann Kohl. Kohl wrote a book about his experiences among the Ojibwa Indians in the middle of the last century.

An old Indian man named Shining Cloud told Kohl about his own vision quest of many years before;

> Grandfather. . . took me by the hand, and led me deep into the forest. Here he selected a lofty tree, a red pine, and prepared a bed for me in the branches, on which I should lie down to fast . . . Then my grandfather said to me that I must on no account take nourishment, neither eat nor drink, pluck no berries, nor even swallow the rainwater that might fall.
>
> The first three or four fast days were. . . terrible. . . and I could not sleep nights for hunger and thirst. But I overcame it, and on the fifth day I felt no more annoyance. I fell into a dreamy and half-paralyzed state, and went to sleep. But only my body slept; my soul was free and awake.
>
> In the first nights nothing happened to me; all was quiet, but on the eighth night I heard a rustling and waving in the branches. It was like a heavy bear or [moose] breaking through the shrubs and forest. I was greatly afraid. I thought there were too many of them, and I made preparations for flight. But the man who approached me, whoever he may have been, read my thoughts and saw my fear at a distance; so he came towards me more and more gently, and rested, quite noiselessly, on the branches over my head.

The spirit then led the young Indian through a series of dream-adventures in which he was made promises.

[He would receive]all the good gifts of God—health, strength, long life,
and all the creatures of nature. Thou shalt become a famous hunter. . .
And that thou mayst avoid illness, receive this box with medicine. Use
it in case of need; and whenever thou art in difficulty, think of [your spirit
helper]. When thou prayest, [I] will help thee, and intercede for thee with
the Master of Life.

Shining Cloud did not awake from his life-dreams until the
tenth day of the vision quest, when he heard the voice of his
grandfather who had come to look for him. 'At home,' Shining
Cloud concludes, 'they prepared for me a soft bed of moss, on
which I lay down like a patient. It was not till the following day
that I took any food, but three days later I was quite recovered,
and strong. And from that time I was, and remained, a perfect
man.'[4]

It is of course ironic that this story should have been recorded
for us by a German who little realized that he was describing a
tradition so similar to one practised by his own pagan ancestors.

Now let us return to the Havamal account. In the second
stanza from the end quoted, 'the son of Bolthorn, Bestla's father'
refers to the god Mimir, called the wisest of the gods. Mimir
was Odin's uncle. He had been killed in a dispute between the
gods before the time depicted in the poem, but apparently came
to Odin as a guardian spirit in his dream.

On many subsequent occasions Odin returned to seek help
and advice from Mimir. On these occasions Odin was always
described as talking to Mimir's disembodied head, but there
is no real need to be literal-minded in understanding what is
meant here; the head of Mimir, the wisest of gods, was probably a symbol of his wisdom.

One more element from the Havamal story of Odin's dream
requires explanation: Othrörir was a drinking horn filled with a
magic mead which conferred the gift of poetry (especially *galdr*,
or sorcerer's poetry). In some places in the mythology, the mead
itself is called Othrörir. See Bragi's discussion with Aegir, quoted
in Chapter 6, for the story of Odin's magic mead of poetry.

We can see how closely the American Indian's narrative of
his experience parallels the Germanic poem in many respects.
Both Odin and Shining Cloud went out to seek their visions
alone, fasting in a treetop. In each case the quest lasted nine
or ten days. Each contacted a spirit-force from whom he received
prophetic knowledge and sacred gifts, and to whom he turned
for aid in times of need throughout later years.

Figure 4: Tenth-century bronze image of Thor, 6.7 cm high, from Eyrarland, Eyjatjörour, Iceland.

PAGAN PRIESTS

In addition to shamans there were two other classes of people who were thought to make regular contact with the unseen world. These were the temple priests and the *volvas*. A priest (called a *godi*) generally specialized in dealing with one specific god such as Frey or Thor, and his job had a recognized economic value; people paid him to make sacrifices to the gods for them. The chieftain (or in Iceland, the administrative head) of an area was often also the *godi*, but this was by no means a universal rule. *Godi* positions could be bought, sold, or passed on as an inheritance. *Godis* were authorized to collect taxes, called *hoftollar*, for the maintenance of their temples. According to surviving written records, the Icelandic *godis* were consecrated into their positions by dipping their hands into the blood of a gelded ram sacrificed for the purpose. Women priestesses, termed *gydjur*, were common especially in the pre-Viking period, and especially in cults devoted to the elves (*disir*) and the spirits of the land (*landvaettir*).

VOLVAS

Volvas were prophetesses and magical practitioners. The *Voluspa*, the poem which opens the Elder Edda, is an extended prophecy given to Odin by a *volva*. In it she first proves her wisdom by telling of the past: of how the world began, of the coming of the Vanir, and of many other things which the gods had thought secret.

> I know where Odin's
>   eye is hidden
> Deep in the wide-famed
>   well of Mimir;
> Mead from the pledge
>   of Odin each morn
> Does Mimir drink:
>   Would you know yet more?

She goes on to tell of what is to come, finally describing how the world will end:

> The giantes sold
>   in ironwood sat
> In the east, and bore
>   the brood of Fenrir;
> Among these one
>   in monster's guise
> Was soon to steal
>   the sun from the sky.

> There feeds he full
>   on the flesh of the dead,
> And the home of the gods
>   he reddens with gore;
> Dark grows the sun,
>   and in summer soon
> Come mighty storms:
>   Would you know yet more?

> Yggdrasil shakes,
>   and shiver on high
> The ancient limbs,
>   and the giant is loose;
> To the head of Mim
>   does Odin give heed,
> But the dark Fenris-wolf
>   Shall slay him soon.

The sun turns black,
  earth sinks in the sea,
The hot stars down
  from heaven are whirled;
Fierce grows the steam
  and the life-feeding flame,
'Til fire leaps high
  about heaven itself.

But in Teutonic mythology the end of the world is not the end of all things, as seems to be commonly thought, for the *volva* goes on:

Now do I see
  the earth anew
Rise all green
  from the waves again;
The cataracts fall,
  and the eagle flies,
And fish he catches
  beneath the cliffs.

The gods in the fields
  meet together,
And talk of the snake
  who belted the earth*,
And the mighty past
  they call to mind,
And the ancient runes
  of the Ruler of Gods.

* The 'snake who belted the earth' is the Midgard-Serpent, whose body went all the way around the world.

   Volvas travelled from settlement with retinues of followers and performed various ceremonies, the best-known of which was the 'high-seat' oracle rite. One of these rites is described in the Vatnsdaela Saga.

   A Viking named Ingjald lived on a prosperous farmstead in the northern part of Heligoland, where he spent his winters quietly, resting from his summer raiding expeditions. Ingjald had as a friend a man named Thorstein Ketilsson and, as was the ancient tradition, he took in his friend's son Ingimund Thorsteinsson to raise him with his own family (a custom called 'fostering', which had the effect of binding the two families together as allies). In this way Ingimund became close friends with his foster brother, Ingjald's son Grim.

   One time a Finnish *volva* came around with her followers and

Ingjald took advantage of the chance to hold a high-seat incantation rite so that he and his men could inquire about their fates (Finns were thought to be especially skilled at prophecy, weather-magic, and certain other kinds of sorcery). The high seat was made ready and a splendid feast was set. Then the witch took her place above the heads of the others, and the men went forward one by one to inquire about their personal futures. She gave each a detailed description of what was coming in his life; some of them were pleased by what the future held and others were not.

Alone among the group, the two foster-brothers kept their seats and did not go forward to hear their prophecies. Noting this, the *volva* asked, 'Why do these two young men not come forward to ask questions of me? Surely they seem the noblest of all in this room.'

Ingimund answered, 'I will find out about my destiny when it comes; I do not care to know about it sooner, and in any case I have no faith in the wagging of thy tongue.'

She then said, 'Bidden or not, I shall tell thee about thy life. Thou wilt go over the seas to find a home in a land called Iceland. Few live there as yet, and there thou wilt rise in rank among men and grow old in fame. Many of thy kin will settle there as well, and will also gain fame in that land.'

'What a remarkable future thou hast foretold for me,' said Ingimund. 'Never shall I set foot in that forsaken land. I should be a feckless son indeed if I were to give up my father's rich lands and sail off into the wilderness.'

The Finnish woman made answer: 'Nevertheless, it will happen as I tell thee. Here is the proof of my words, as thou shalt see in due time. King Harald gave thee a silver amulet with Frey's image upon it. That medal which the King gave thee in Havrsfjord is no longer in thy purse. Already it lies on a stone ridge in that far land where thou shalt make thy home. When thou findest it there years hence, thou shalt think of me and know how I spoke the truth.'

Ingimund then said, 'If thou wert not under my foster father's home and sheltered by his hospitality I would pay thee for thy prophecy by knocking thee off that high seat. But I am an easygoing man and pride myself on how I keep rein over my temper, so I shall not strike thee.'

'Be not angry with me,' said the *volva*. 'It will be as I say whether thou likest it or not. And thou mayest as well know that the fate of Grim points also to Iceland, as does that of his brother Hromund. Both will become great freeholders out there.' Next morning Ingimund searched frantically for his Frey-medallion but could not find it anywhere.

Ingimund went on to become a great Viking and raided the British Isles many times. When King Harald (who had previously been only a petty king in a small realm) was fighting his way to power over all Norway, Ingimund took his side against a man named Thorir Long-Chin and defeated him in battle. Harald rewarded Ingimund with a large haul of war booty and gave him Thorir's daughter for a wife.

Because Ingimund had made so many enemies fighting for Harald, the king suggested that he would be wise to take his new wife and wealth out of the country and seek his destiny in Iceland. Ingimund said again, as he had years before in his father's house, that he had never intended to go there, but all the same he engaged two Lapplander sorcerers to go into a trance and send their souls out to find out what they could. When they returned to consciousness they said that their spirits had gone to Iceland, where they travelled to a certain valley between two hills. There they could magically see a silver medallion lying buried in the soil. It had an image of Frey on it. They then gave a detailed description of how the land lay in that region.

With this sign Ingimund gave up his resistance and set out for Iceland with a party of relatives and friends. After much travel over the island, he was able to find a valley which matched the description given him by the Lappish wizards. There he settled and, while he was digging the foundation for his private temple, he found the Frey medal which the king had given him so many years before.

The most detailed description we have of a high-seat ritual occurs in *Eiriks Saga Rauda* (otherwise known as the saga of Eric the Red, which also contains the story of Leif Ericson's voyage to North America).

This story occurred at an Icelandic settlement in Greenland at a time when there was a terrible famine. Fishing and foraging expeditions were coming back empty-handed, and some did not manage to return at all. A woman named Thorbjorg in the community had a reputation as a *volva*. She had done many foretellings for people and so Thorkel the headman asked her to come to his home and prophesy when the troubles would end. He prepared a high-seat for her as required, with a cushion stuffed with hen feathers.

Thorbjorg arrived that evening with her escort. She was dressed in a blue cloak decorated with many stones. She wore a necklace of glass beads and a black lambskin hood which was trimmed with white cat fur. She brandished a staff which was encrusted with stones and topped with a brass knob. A bag of magical charms hung from the belt at her waist. Her hands were covered with catskin gloves which were made with the white fur turned inward, and on her feet she wore leather boots with the hair still attached.

The *volva* then greeted everyone in the room and sat down to a ritual meal of goat's milk gruel and meat from the hearts of all the various animals that could be obtained there. The knife she used had a handle of walrus ivory, and her spoon was brass. When she was done she said she could have no answer to Thorkel's questions until the next day.

The next afternoon the procedure got underway again. Thorbjorg readied her materials and then requested the help of any women who knew the spells necessary for doing sorcery. When it turned out that none among those present could help her, the call went out among the other settlers. Finally a woman named Gudrid admitted that her foster-mother had taught her warlock songs back in Iceland, but she wanted nothing to do with Thorbjorg's ceremony because she was a Christian. Thorbjorg appealed to her host Thorkel, saying that the foretelling could not go on without Gudrid's help. Thorkel was finally able to pressure the reluctant woman into working with the *volva*.

Thorbjorg mounted the dais to her high seat, the other women gathered around, and Gudrid sang the witching songs she had learned in childhood. The *volva* thanked her and said:

> The multitude of spirits are now here. The singing has brought them and won their good will. They are now showing me what was hidden before.
> The famine will soon end, and with it the disease that has ravaged among us. Spring will soon come to these lands, and with it the end to our torment.
> And you, Gudrid: I see a most bright future for you. Soon you will marry well here in Greenland, and shortly thereafter you will go back to Iceland to begin a family line that will rise to fame. The spirits will look kindly upon your descendants down through the years. Goodbye to you, my daughter.

Then the others came forward to have their fortunes told, each asking what he or she most wished to know. Thorbjorg answered all of these questions one by one, and the saga writer assures us that 'there were few things which did not turn out as she prophesied'.

THE ELDER AND THE YOUNGER RUNES

If you tried to read any of the runic stones depicted in this book or elsewhere, you may have noticed that some of them contain letters which look different from the runes which form the basis of discussion in these pages. This circumstance deserves some discussion.

In most of the Germanic world the Futhark underwent few changes from the time of its origin until the advance of Christianity brought in Roman letters to displace it. In Scandinavia, however, where Christianity made no significant inroads until about the year 1000, something quite remarkable happened to the runes. Beginning in about AD600 people began to experiment with various modifications to the Futhark. The changes were of two kinds. First, the shapes of many of the letters were simplified; and second, several letters were eliminated. Some of these letters had simply fallen into disuse due to language changes, but not all. The net effect of these changes seems to have been to create an abbreviated form of the Futhark. By AD 800-850 the changes were complete and the resultant 'younger' runes were in use throughout Scandinavia just in time for the opening of the Viking era.

These alterations were very systematic. First, the so-called 'elder runes', the original twenty-four rune Futhark, contained two characters, < and ◇, which were smaller than the rest. ◇ was eliminated and < was given a new shape, ᚴ, making its length consistent witht he rest of the rune-row.

ᚻ, ᛗ, ᛗ and N are all 'two-stave' runes which contain two vertical shafts. ᛗ and ᛗ were dropped and the two remaining characters were simplified into one-stave forms, becoming ᛒ and ᚤ, respectively.

Six more letters were discarded and changes occurred in both the forms and sound-values of other letters. For example, the Scandinavian languages lost the initial j in many words. The word for 'year', originally JARA, became AR. The associated rune (ᛡ) acquired the new form ᛆ and changed from representing the J-sound to A. Meanwhile, the pronunciation of the word for 'god' had evolved across the years from ANSUZ to OSS and the ᚠ-rune changed in sound from A to O in parallel with the language change. ᛟ, the old O-rune, thus became redundant and was lost. Also, some of the rune names changed at this time. URUZ (Aurochs) became UR (Rain), etc.

Further evidence of a systematic deletion process lies in the observation that there were three pairs of runes in the old alphabet in which the members of each pair differed phonetically only in that one was voiced and the other voiceless. These pairs were ᚲ-ᚷ, ᛈ-ᛒ, and ᛏ-ᛞ (K-G, P-B, and T-D). One element of each pair was among the runes discarded, and the other element was subsequently used to represent both sounds.

Especially odd is what happened to ᛉ, the Z-rune: they not only inverted it (ᛣ) but moved it out of its traditional position to the end of the alphabet and changed its meaning from ALGIZ, 'elk' (moose) to YR, 'Yew' (YR being the linguistic descendant of the earlier word IWAZ). In some forms of the 16-rune alphabet the M-rune then inherited the ᛉ-shape.

Table 1 summarizes the changes which occurred.

Table 1: The old and new runes

AETT	Old	New	Letter Value	Old Form	New Form
1 or 3	1	1	F	ᚠ	ᚡ
	2	2	U	ᚢ	ᚢ
	3	3	Th	ᚦ	ᚦ
	4	4	A (O)	ᚨ	ᚭ
	5	5	R	ᚱ	ᚱ
	6	6	K	ᚲ	ᚤ
	7		G	ᚷ	
	8		W	ᚹ	
2	1	1	H	ᚺ	ᚼ
	2	2	N	ᚾ	ᚾ
	3	3	I	ᛁ	ᛁ
	4	4	J (A)	ᛃ	ᛅ
	5		Eh	ᛇ	
	6		p	ᛈ	
	7		z	ᛉ	
	8	5	S	ᛋ	ᛌ
3 or 1	1	1	T	ᛏ	ᛏ
	2	2	B	ᛒ	ᛒ
	3		E	ᛖ	
	4	3	M	ᛗ	ᛘ
	5	4	L	ᛚ	ᛚ
	6		Ng	ᛜ	
	7		D	ᛞ	
	8		O	ᛟ	
		5	Z		ᛣ

The reasons for this sweeping change are not clear—although the change itself its strangely reminiscent of the 'reforms' of lan-

guage, spelling, and alphabet which the Scandinavians period-
ically subject themselves to, even to this day—Denmark having
last tinkered with its alphabet just after the Second World War,
at which time they made the double letter AA into a single letter
Å and (as you might guess) moved it from the beginning to the
end of the alphabet.

Two further complications remain: there were four or five
different styles of writing the younger runes. These variant forms
all contain the same letters in the same order as are shown in the
column for the New Forms in Table 1, and the variations among
them are purely stylistic or calligraphic, having no more significance than do the various typefaces in which we are

Figure 5: The Rök Stone — East Gotland, Sweden, AD900.
The Rök style of Younger Runes is named for this stone, which has the longest
message of any known runic monument. In addition to Rök-style runes, portions
of the text are carved in runes from the elder 24-rune alphabet and in the 'tent'
and 'twig' types of secret runes.

The message begins 'These runes stand in memory of Waemoth, written by
Warin, a father, to commemorate his dead son, and then goes on to refer to various heroic and legendary deeds, with the apparent intention of inspiring young
warriors to go forth and emulate them. The text closes with the words 'Let us tell
the young men: strike boldly. Biari is priest at the temple, a wise rune-carver'.

accustomed to seeing our own Roman alphabet printed.

These variations in letter styles tend to obscure the remarkable uniformity which arose once again in the runic tradition. Relatively suddenly, after two centuries of near chaos, in about AD800 everyone across the pagan Scandinavian world was writing in the same new set of letters. There was no unifying political or religious mechanism to mandate this rise of a new orthodoxy, nor any compelling reason one can think of why the new rune system should have been so universally accepted: indeed, as we shall shortly see, the new alphabet was in certain ways inferior to the old one as a vehicle for writing the Norse language.

Table 1 shows the most widespread of the new Futhark styles, commonly called the Danish runes. Below are three other calligraphic styles, usually termed Norwegian, Rök (Figure 3), and Staveless, respectively:

Norwegian:	ᚦ	ᚢ	ᚦ	ᚨ	ᚱ	ᚲ	ᚼ	ᚾ	ᛁ	ᛅ	ᚼ	ᛏ	ᛒ	ᛦ	ᛚ	ᛣ
Rök:	ᚦ	ᚢ	ᚦ	ᚴ	ᚱ	ᚲ	ᛏ	ᚼ	ᛁ	ᚱ	ᛁ	ᛏ	ᚠ	ᛏ	ᚼ	ᛁ
Staveless:															:	:
	F	U	Th	A	R	K	H	N	I	A	S	T	B	M	L	Z

The Staveless characters took the reductionist impulse about as far as it would go. With the vertical staves removed, these runes had to be written between top and bottom boundary lines to show the relative positions, top middle or bottom, of the little branches which were now all that was left to represent the letters.

The second complication derives from the fact that, after all the changes were made, the result was a set of letters less adequate to writing the Viking dialects than was the original Futhark. As a result, later users of the Futhark were obliged to create additional runes, which they did by adding dots to some of th existing characters: ᚢ (dotted UR) for 'Y', ᚴ (dotted KAUN) for 'G', ᛂ (dotted ISAZ) for 'Eh', ᛏ (dotted TYR) for 'D' and ᛒ (dotted BJARKAN) for 'P'.

It was these dotted runes that were absorbed into Christian custom (along with the Christmas tree, the Yule log, and the Easter egg, all of which also had nordic pagan origins). Christian priests used the runes for ecclesiastical calendars and many of the older churches in Scandinavia have runic blessings carved into their walls and altars. Grave monuments of Christian kings, nobles, and churchmen continued to be carved with runic inscriptions.

The runes remained in constant use in parts of Norway and Sweden until relatively recent times. As late as the latter part of the nineteenth century, when villagers in some of the more remote parishes advertised for a pastor they specified that they wanted someone who could 'read and write the runes'.

THE KENSINGTON STONE

From time to time runic carvings have surfaced in North America, the most famous of these being the 'Kensington Stone' found at Kensington, Minnesota. Controversy still rages over whether these artifacts are recent forgeries or authentic evidence that Vikings were in the interior of the continent in the thirteenth or fourteenth century. Whatever they finally turn out to be, they were carved in a system based on the 'Dotted Runes'.

It is no part of our present purpose to enter into this debate, but it is interesting to note what happened when the inscription of the Kensington stone was reproduced in midwestern

Figure 6: The Kensington rune store is now displayed in the Rune Stone Museum, Alexandria, Minnesota.

Scandinavian-language newspapers shortly after it was discovered. Within a few days of its appearance, the papers received
at least three competent translations of the runes from their
readers in Minnesota alone. We can see from this incident that
knowledge of the runes was quite widespread among the Scandinavian immigrants. An obvious corollary of this fact is that
there were also a number of people in Minnesota who would have
been capable of *creating* a runic forgery.

2. THE MAGICAL MINDSET

Opdage in the old Icelandic-Norwegian language
particularly meant 'surprise trolls at daybreak'.
—William Thalbitzer

To the ancient Germanic peoples, the world was a magical place, a place far different from the inert, mechanical universe which their descendants inhabit. In addition to the major gods, there were other strange beings and mysterious forces abroad in the land in those days.

SPIRITS OF THE LAND

The *landvaettir* were simple, shy spirits of the soil, generally thought to live in groves, mounds, waterfalls, and similar geographic features. In some traditions they were equated with the spirits of the dead. They could only be seen by those who possessed second sight. It was on their account that the famous dragon heads of viking ships were made so they could be removed from the forward peak of the ship. Common tradition as well as Icelandic law considered it a grave offence to sail into a friendly port with the dragon's head mounted at the prow because the fearsome image might frighten away the *landvaettir* and therefore spoil the fruitfulness of the land. In Egil's Saga it is told how when Egil became angered at the Norwegian king he set up a 'scorning post' and directed it not only against the royal court but also against 'those

Figure 7: Rune stone at Ramsund, Södermaland, Sweden, depicts scenes from the Sigurd (Siegfried) legend. Sigurd kills the dragon, Fafnir, roasts its heart, and sucks his burnt thumb.

landvaettir who live in this land, that they may all became lost and not find their way back until the king and his wife be driven from their realm.'

GUARDIAN SPIRITS

There were female spirit-forces generically called *disir*. They were ruled by Freya and worshipped by mankind with sacrificial rituals (*disablot*). The *nornir* (Norns), were one type of *disir*. They were guardian spirits who controlled human destinies and looked after the fortunes of individuals and families. The Norns were often imagined as spinning out the fates of humans like flaxen threads. When the thread came to an end the person died. Perhaps this metaphor lingers in the word 'distaff' (*Dis*-staff), which originally meant a rod used in spinning flax.

There were three principal Norns named Urth, Verthandi, and Skuld (Past, Present, and Future) associated with the world-tree Yggdrasil, the same tree whose roots reach into all the worlds, where Mimir dwells and where Odin sought his shamanistic vision.

> An ash I know,
>   Yggdrasil its name,
> With water white
>   is the great tree wet.
> Thence come the dews

that fall in the dales,
Green by Urth's well
  does it ever grow.
Thence come the maidens
  mighty in wisdom
Three from the dwelling
  down 'neath the tree;
Urth is one named,
  Verthandi the next——
On the wood they scored——
  and Skuld the third.
Laws they made there,
  and life allotted
To the sons of men,
  and set their fates.

                  —Voluspa

Offerings were made to the Norns in behalf of a child when it was born, and the Norns were supposed to show their good-will to the child by putting *Nornaspor*, white marks, on its fingernails. The white marks were believed to bring good luck.

Of different origin are the Norns,
Not all of one race.
Some are of the people of the Aesir,
Some are of the people of the Alfar,
And some are Dvalinn's* daughters.

*Dvalinn was a dwarf. See the section on dwarfs.

Figure 8: Sixth-century silver figures, 3 cm tall, probably of Valkyries, found at Öland, Sweden. Valkyries were said to serve at Valahalla when the souls of brave Vikings who died in battle feasted and drank.

The Prose Edda tells about an occasion when a mortal was talking with Odin. 'If it is the Norns who shape men's fates, then they are hardly even-handed in the destinies they create for them. Some men live full and prosperous lives, while others are denied fortune and glory. Some live to be gray-beards while others are cut down in youth.'

Odin replied, 'The benificent Norns who come from good family lineages create good lives for people, but folk who live out lives of sorrow and misfortune owe it to mean-spirited and evil Norns.'

The Valkyries, who carried fallen warriors from the battle-field to Valhalla, were also classified as *disir*. A hero dying on the battlefield sings:

> Home bid me the Valkyries,
> Who from high Valhall,
> Odin hither sent to me.
> Gladly ale with Aesir
> Shall I drink in high-seat.

Figure 9: Store at Hunnestad, Skane, Sweden, depicts a giantess riding on a wolf, which she guides using serpents for reins and riding crop.

GIANTS

Giants, or ogres, were enemies of both gods and men. Shaggy, monstrous beasts, they were sometimes many-headed and were thought able to alter their shapes. Ugly as the males of the species were, the females were often beautiful and much in demand as mates for the gods and heroes. It was sometimes said that the giants, like the dwarfs, could be turned to stone by exposure to sunlight. There were frost-giants, who personified ice and snow and controlled freezing seas, glaciers, icecaps, and icebergs; fire-giants, who controlled volcanic eruptions, lightning, and the northern lights; hill-giants who controlled rockslides, earthquakes, and landslips; forest-giants, who inhabited the wild places where they threatened those who would cut down their trees; and water-giants, who personified the dangers of the flood. Grendel and his mother, the monsters of the Beowulf poem, were of this sort. All giants were cannibals. They dwelt in their own land, Jotunheim, from where it was thought that they will come forth to battle against the gods at the time of the *Götterdämmerung* (Twilight of the Gods), the great war at the end of the world.

ELVES

There were elves about; not the reclusive little tricksters of Celtic fable, but powerful creatures allied with gods and ruled by Frey, who lived with them in Alfheim. They shared in the feasts of the gods and were considered worthy of sacrificial rituals (*Alfablot*) in their own right, as were the *disir*. Such rites were conducted at mounds which were associated with them.

Snorri writes of them in the Prose Edda:

> There is a place called Alfheim, and there dwell the people called the light elves, while the dark elves dwell in the earth beneath. Most unlike are these two, even more so in their natures than in their appearance. The light elves are fairer than sunlight, but the dark ones are blacker than tar.

There was an elf cult in Sweden, where they were apparently venerated along with Frey. In Kormak's Saga we read how Kormak wounded a man named Thorvard in a fight. Thorvard's wound was slow to heal so he went to a witch named Thordis. She told him: 'Near here there is a hill in which the elves live. Kormak has just killed a bull. You must get that bull and stain the elf-hill red with its blood, and use its meat to make a feast for the elves. Then you will recover your health'.

DWARFS

Dwarfs were related to the elves. Skilled and magical metal-workers, cunning sorcerers endowed with secret knowledge, they could not stand the sun—the light could turn them to stone—so they lived underground in a lavish kingdom, coming out only at night. They worked gold into the treasures of the gods and sometimes made weapons for men. Dvalinn was the most famous of the dwarfs. It was he who made Odin's spear and Frey's magic ship, Skidbladnir, which could sail the sky as easily as the water, which could always catch a favourable wind, and which, though it could carry all the gods and their horses, would yet fold up small enough to fit in a pocket. The warrior-poet Egil Skallagrimsson, subject of Egils Saga, had a sword made by the dwarfs. Egil had lost his hand but this sword had been so cleverly wrought that he could fasten it to his elbow and wield it as well as if his hand still grasped it. The Norwegians call echoes *dvergamal* (dwarf speech) because the mountain dwarfs were thought to throw one's words back to him.

MAGICAL POWER

More fundamental than the various gods, ogres, and fertility-spirits was the idea of *megin*. *Megin* is a force which pervades the universe, possessed in varying degree by every person, animal, rock, plant, and twig. It is the hidden power which gives strength to men as well as gods. Earthquakes, storms, and volcanoes are all displays of *megin*. If a person succumbs to a disease, the *megin* of the disease is proved stronger than that of its victim.

The concept of *megin* is identical to the *mana* of the South Sea Islanders, *ch'i* of the Chinese, the *maxpey* of the Crow, and the *njomm* of the Ekoi Indians. *Megin*, like its equivalent in the other cultures, has certain definite attributes, among which is its ability to be transferred from one person or thing to another. A noteworthy example may be found in the case of the legendary Berserkers. They were a special class

Figure 10: A Berserk and a warrior in a wolf skin, depicted on a stamp for making impressions on bronze plates (Uppland, Sweden).

of Viking warriors, known for their ability to enter a state of mindless, explosive fury when in combat. Their name comes from 'baer-serk', or bear-shirt, because the berserkers wore bearskins and dined ritually on bear meat in order to acquire the savage strength of the animal.

Thor had a magic belt, *Megingjardar*, which gave him special strength when he wore it, just as Odin had a magic spear in which resided his power to grant victory in battles among mortals. On those occasions when the weaker combatant killed the stronger, the people said it was because Odin intervened with his spear to claim the better man for his army in Valhalla. Odin recited charms over the head of the dead god Mimir so it would become animate and speak to him when he needed its sage advice.

A traditional Polynesian Islander should he be familiar with bicycles, would say that a fast, well-made bicycle has more *mana* than an inefficient machine. A wise or physically powerful man has more *mana* than a stupid or weak one; a well-constructed canoe that glides easily through the water has greater *mana* than does a clumsy craft which wallows in the sea. Likewise, *megin* means 'power' whether one is referring to a warrior's might or to *asmegin*, the power of the gods.

Humans, as well as the gods can, control *megin* through magic, charms, sacrifices, and rites. By these various means one can *magna* objects, or charge them with *megin*. There are ways of making stones into amulets (*magna steina*), ways of activating rune magic, and so on. A synonym for *magnat* (past tense of *magna*) is *aukinn*, or 'augmented'. An image of Thor was said to have become so *magnat* by the sacrifices made to it that it came alive and walked about.

Atheists were not uncommon among the Germanic peoples. An Upplandic chieftain named Bard spoke for many of them when he said, 'I hold no belief in either the altars of the gods nor in demons. I have made my way from realm to realm and have met giants as well as black men, but I have proved their equal and more'. Like the Danish king Hrolf Kraki, these men held that fate rather than the gods controlled their lives, and believed only in their own strength—and, most interestingly, in *megin* (*a matt sin ok megin*). The concept of the universal mind-force was so deeply ingrained in their philosophical outlook that even those who rejected the gods never thought of giving up the theory of an animate universe.

3. THE SORCERER'S UNIVERSE

In general, human societies may be divided into *vitalistic* cultures: those which assume a spiritual component to things in the external world, and *materialistic* cultures: those which attribute purely physical or mechanistic traits to those portions of the world which are not (to them) obviously alive. The distinction between vitalism and materialism is an important one in the present discussion because magical beliefs are universal in vitalistic cultures and nonexistent, or nearly so, in materialistic ones.

Vitalistic beliefs are of two general types, which the anthropologists call *animism* and *animatism*. Animism is a belief in discrete, individual spirits, such as the *landvaetter, disir,* elves, etc. discussed above. Animatism, on the other hand, is the belief that there is an animating principle, an element of consciousness, in all things: *mana* or *megin*, in other words. Obviously, one can believe in the spirit-world and in a force such as *megin* at the same time, as did the old Germanic peoples, and as do many other peoples of the world.

The animist conceives the individual spirits of his belief as each having an independent will or purposefulness. The purposes of the individual spirits may be aligned with or against those of a given human being, and spirits may be allied or antagonistic toward each other. *Megin* (or *mana*), on the other hand, is generally thought of as a more rudimentary sort of psychism, devoid of will of its own but capable of manipulation by spirit-forces or by humans who have the proper skills. Animatism is therefore the more parsimonious of the two theories; that is, it makes fewer assumptions, or hypothesizes fewer entities, in its explanation of events.

Each culture makes assumptions about the nature of reality and teaches its members to think of and perceive the world in accordance with those assumptions. In the depths of our ethnocentrism, we mistake our own philosophical prejudices for the right and proper order of things. We readily forget that the distinction which we make between the natural and the supernatural is a recent invention of European culture, probably not much (if at all) older than the Enlightenment period of the seventeenth and eighteenth centuries, when the apparent success of Newtonian physics began to lead philosophers into the belief that the whole of the material universe could be explained with mechanical laws and without recourse to notions of divine (or diabolical) intervention.

The old Germanic world-view did not make a division between the mundane and the miraculous, nor do most other human belief systems. The true importance of this distinction is that one must classify those phenomena which we call 'supernatural' as out of the ordinary before the declaration can be made that they are impossible.

A DREAM THEORY OF VITALISM

How, we may ask, does it happen that so many people through the centuries and across the continents have come to hold these peculiar beliefs? The earliest anthropological explanation for animism was advanced by E. B. Tyler in 1871. As McDougall explains this theory, the belief in external consciousness arises from primitive man's experience with dreams and his need to explain how 'in sleep, while the body lies at rest [and] the sleeper remains unconscious of the surroundings of his body he seems to himself to visit other scenes, to meet and converse with other persons, and to have the use in these dream-adventures of his dress and weapons'.

> In visions, and in dreams [primitive man] sees, too, the shadowy forms of dead friends. Since, then, most savages regard their dream-experiences as equally real with those of waking life, they naturally and inevitably arrive at the theory that the ghost-self, which in dreams can appear in distant places, leaving the deserted body in deathlike stillness, is identical with the animating principle.

Other theorists have added that waking hallucinations and similar phenomena undoubtedly contributed to the development of the ghost-soul concept.

McDougall continues:

> The ascription by primitive men of ghost-souls to animals, plants, and inert objects, is probably. . . an extension of the theory first arrived at by reflection on the problem of human life. Such extension was rendered almost inevitable by the fact that persons met in dreams and visions, as well as the dreamer himself, seem to have about them their dogs, their weapons, their dress, and other material objects. It seems probable that the ghost-soul of man was the first definite conception of personal intelligent powers, living and working in detachment from ordinary solid matter and all the narrow limitations of embodied existence. If so, the developments of ideas about other powers of a similar, but non-human, nature, demons, gods, spirits of good and evil of all sorts, must have been in large degree merely extensions and differentiations of this fundamental notion of the human ghost-soul.[5]

In fact, though, we now know that vitalist ideas occur naturally and spontaneously during the development of every human child.

A DEVELOPMENT VIEW OF VITALISM

A more adequate explanation of the origins of vitalism owes much to the developmental psychology of Swiss theorist Jean Piaget. Piaget wrote a large and diffuse body of works in which he described the development of children's mental processes. One of his most important early findings was that all young children are vitalists.

At birth (according to Piaget and most other psychologists before and since), the human infant knows only consciousness. She is aware of her own mind and the perceptions and rudimentary emotions which impress themselves upon it, but there is no awareness of a boundary between what is inside that consciousness and what is outside. As Piaget put it, 'Since the child does not distinguish the psychical from the physical world, since in the early stages of his development he does not even recognize any definite limits between himself and the outside world, it is to be expected that he will regard as living and conscious a large number of objects which are for us inert'. The child, Piaget says, 'confuses himself with the Universe'. He is not, for example, aware that he is hungry, but only that the Cosmos is filled with the sensation of hunger.

One of the first steps the child must take in rising out of this primitive state is to learn the fundamental boundary in his world: that which separates what is inside him from what is outside. This discrimination between the self and nonself undoubtedly comes about naturally as he discovers he can move limbs with his thoughts, but (at least in the ordinary course of events) he will forever remain unable to move certain other parts of the world, such as the furniture, by simply wishing it; as he learns, in other words, that his arm is part of him and subject to his will while the dining-room table is not.

When a child discovers this boundary between herself and everything else, she does not automatically learn that the things outside are essentially different from what is inside her. She has direct knowledge of her own consciousness, and it is natural for her to assume that the things outside are also conscious. By way of analogy: when a farmer puts up a fence around his property he is merely claiming possession of the territory within the fence; he is not asserting that the land inside is fundamentally different from the realms beyond his gate.

Piaget's fundamental method was to talk to children about their ideas, and his most important early research subjects were his own children. He tracked the evolution of their ideas and cognitive skills through childhood, finding them to pass through four stages of animistic thinking on their way to adulthood.

In the first phase, the child responds to all useful or unbroken objects as if they were alive. Among Piaget's young European subjects this stage lasted until about age seven. Here is a discussion Piaget had with one of his children at that age: 'If you pricked this stone, would it feel it? *No.* Why not? *Because it is hard.* If you put it in the fire, would it feel it? *Yes.* Why? *Because it would get burnt.* Can it feel the cold or hot? *Yes.*'[6]

As Piaget summarizes, 'the child endows all things with consciousness, but not with consciousness of everything. . . Having no notion of a possible distinction between thought and physical objects, he does not realize that there can be actions unaccompanied by consciousness'.

In the next stage children generally stop attributing awareness to things like rocks, houses, and furniture. However, they still treat things 'ordinarily in motion or whose special function is to be in motion' as conscious. 'Thus', Piaget says, 'the sun and moon, the stars, clouds, rivers, the wind, carts, fire, etc., are all regarded as conscious. . . In fact, children either attribute consciousness to everything [Stage I] or they attribute it to things which move, as if all movement implied voluntary effort [Stage II]'.

But this second stage is transitory, for children 'soon realize that the movement of certain things, such as that of a bicycle, comes entirely from the outside , from the man pedalling for example. As soon as this distinction is made, the child restricts consciousness to things that can move of their own accord, and thus reaches the third stage'.

In Stage III, which begins at about age nine, children still allow consciousness to the sun and moon, wind, clouds, and streams because these things move without any apparent human intervention. The child says that they move because they want to. It is not until about age twelve that children in western society enter Stage IV, reconciling themselves to the dominant opinion of the adults around them that only humans and some animals have consciousness.

Parallels can easily be shown between the animism of western children and that of various non-western peoples. For instance, Hallowell points out the following:

> [The Ojibwa have no] notion of the ordered regularity which is inherent in our scientific outlook. [They] entertain no reasonable certainty that, in accordance with natural law, the sun will 'rise' day after day. . . Any regularity in the movements of the sun is the same order as the habitual activities of human beings. There are certain expectations, of course, but, on occasion, there may be temporary deviations in behaviour 'caused' by other persons. Above all, any concept of *impersonal* 'natural' forces is totally foreign to Ojibwa thought.[7]

The sun rises, in other words, because it wants to.

Some theorists conclude from cross-cultural observations that peoples who hold vitalistic views are victims of arrested development, that they have failed to progress properly through the cognitive stages which lead to a fully adult conception of reality. The hidden assumption in this interpretation of vitalism is that there is something 'natural' or necessary about the sequence of events which Piaget described, but this assumption is not correct. What Piaget has actually described is the long, difficult process through which the western child must pass before he can finally be made to reject the intuitively obvious concept of an animate universe in favour of the mechanistic theories of the society into which he is born. The fact that this anti-vitalist indoctrination process occurs throughout a period when the child is making rapid and profound gains in cognitive skills has led theorists to the faulty conclusion that the child's philosophical shift away from vitalism is strictly due to his growth in mental ability.

The child in every society learns to make the self-nonself discrimination, for the nature of things soon makes it obvious that there is a part of the universe which is under the child's direct control and awareness: its own consciousness and body, and a part which is not under the immediate influence of its will: namely, the rest of the world. However, there would not seem to be any experiment one could perform to determine whether or not a rock, a tree, a bicycle, or the sun has feelings like one's own.

The western child learns to accept the inert and wholly material nature of these things solely on the authority of the adults around him. Adults in modern Europe and America correct children who say that a rock feels pain or rolls down hill because it wants to. They do not correct children who say that Aunt Mabel might want a new dress for Christmas, that Uncle Charlie looks angry, or that the dog wants to go outside. Thus, children eventually learn that it is permissible to think that Aunt Mabel, Uncle Charlie, and the dog are conscious, but wrong to suppose that rocks or trees share in this attribute.

However, vitalistic societies teach different ideas of reality. They do not put their children through twelve difficult years of counterintuitive instruction in attributing consciousness only to humans and animals. Rather, they accept the primal belief that consciousness pervades the universe, and then go on to teach various theories concerning the nature of that consciousness.

Thus Polynesian children learn about the doctrine of *mana*, while Ojibwa Indian children are taught that there is a *manitou* (spirit) of the sun, another of flint, another which oversees the deer, and so on. The Ojibwa leave food at the graves of their dead to sustain them on the long path to heaven. It is obvious to these Indians that the dead do not eat this food; in fact, there is no taboo against removing food from one of these graves. The dead are nourished by the spirit-essence of the food, not by the food itself.

The point here is that, though the children of vitalistic societies learn to make the distinction between themselves and the outside world, their elders do not force upon them the *untestable conclusion* that the phenomenon of consciousness is limited only to their side of the boundary (and to other people and animals). This is the crucial factor which allows these people to adopt a theory of the universe in which magic is plausible.

If it should turn out that magic does exist, then we may well discover that the proper question is not 'Whatever gives those savages the crazy idea that rocks can think?' but rather 'Why does western man reject something which every child knows: that there is consciousness at large in the universe?'

SOME LAWS OF MIND

It is but a tiny step from the belief that the outside world is permeated with consciousness to the suspicion that events outside oneself sometimes follow the same laws one knows to operate inside one's own mind. Vitalists invariably take this step.

The pioneering genius of American psychology, William James, described three connecting principles of thought in the stream of consciousness. The first and *least* important of these principles is analogous to ordinary causation, in which 'the mind proceeds from one object to another by some rational path of connection', as when the need to open a door makes you try to remember where you left your keys, or when an ominous noise coming out from under the hood of your car makes you review what you know of auto mechanics.

But, writes James, 'reason is only one of a thousand possibilities in the thinking of each of us. Who can count all the silly fancies, the utterly irrelevant reflections he makes in the course of a day?' He goes on to make the case that these 'thousand possibilities' may all be accounted for with two further laws of association. The first of these is the law of *contiguity*:

> Objects once experienced together tend to become associated in the imagination, so that when any one of them is thought of, the others are likely to be thought of also, in the same order of sequence or coexistence as before.[8]

A common instance of contiguity occurs when lovers adopt a given tune as 'their song' because it was associated with some romantic moment in their past. Hearing the song again brings that magic moment back in memory. Or, more prosaically, the smell of frying bacon may lead to thoughts of eggs, a frying pan, or a dining-room because of the frequent continuous associations among these items.

We all have intuitive knowledge of the law of contiguity, and we often attempt to capitalize on its action in trying to prompt our recall of some specific information. For instance, suppose that you recognize someone at a party but can't remember her name or anything about her. You might try to recall the circumstances under which you first met her, hoping by that means to bring back the missing name. In like fashion, students have been known to go into an examination hall to study before a test in hopes that learning the material in the same place where they will have to recall it might give them specific memory cues and help their test performance.

One very effective parlour trick for memorizing lists of up to ten things works as follows: first, the performer learns a list of ten 'anchor' objects, each of which is paired with a number between one and ten. The associations between the numbers and the anchors is assisted by rhymes: one-bun; two-shoe; three-tree; four-door; five-hive; six-sticks; seven-heaven; eight-gate; nine; ten-den. This list the performer keeps permanently in memory, having practised visualizing the bun, shoe, tree, etc as vividly as possible. The audience must then name ten objects slowly, one by one. Suppose the first object named is an elephant. He would then perhaps imagine an elephant clamped in a huge hamburger bun. The next thing to be named might be an umbrella. He could visualize a folded umbrella tucked into an old shoe, and so on down the list. When he wants to recall the first item he thinks of the bun, and the silly image of an elephant sandwiched in the bun springs to mind. This stunt makes very efficient use of the principle of contiguity; with a little practice almost anyone can become very good at it.

James's second law is *similarity*, wherein a given thought will tend to attract into consciousness thoughts of similar things. For example, a woman thinking of giving her child a dog might drift into a reverie about the dog she had owned in her own childhood. We use this law too when we try to prompt our memory. Surely you have had the frustrating experience of having a word 'on the tip of your tongue'. In trying to retrieve it, you probably thought of synonyms, of words and phrases near to it in meaning, trying to bring the missing word to mind. In this case you were trying to take advantage of the similarity principle.

In addition to the laws of contiguity and similarity, there is another principle at work in forming and activating associations: the law of *arousal* or emotionality. What is your earliest memory? Odds are, it is connected with some intense emotional experience in your early childhood. Or again, almost everyone old enough to remember President Kennedy's assassination can tell you exactly where he was at the moment when he first heard about that tragic event. The associative connection between the commonplace activities and the fateful events of that day are indelibly burnt into memory because of the intense emotions which people experienced then.

It is said that many years ago in England, before accurate surveying methods were widespread, the landholders devised a unique way of permanently locating property corners. Once the interested parties had agreed on where the corner was to be marked, they took a small peasant boy to the spot and thrashed him within an inch of his life. For the rest of his life that boy was the undisputed authority on the precise location of the corner: it was taken for granted that he would never forget the exact place where he got his beating.

IMPLICATIONS OF VITALISM

People everywhere have accepted the idea of causal connections between events, even though they may not customarily phrase these relationships in the terse language of western science. Likewise, western materialists, who cling to the doctrine that ordinary causal connections are the only sort of links there are between things that happen in the external world, accept the idea that their own minds operate associatively, which is to say that their ideas are connected to one another through contiguity and similarity, and that these bonds can be strengthened by repetition and by the presence of higher arousal states.

Where the vitalists and the materialists differ is that the vitalists not only believe in causal chains, but also expect the mental laws of contiguity, similarity and arousal to operate between events in the external world as well as within their own minds. This difference of opinion is the major practical consequence of the vitalist's assertion, and the materialist's denial, of a mindlike force such as *mana* or *megin* at large in the universe.

For example, when a materialist is confronted with one of life's strange coincidences, he can scratch his head and either forget about it or recount the incident to amaze his friends. In either case, the coincidence has no place in his world-view. To a vitalist, however, coincidences, telepathy, clairvoyance, precognition and the like are simply manifestations of order in the universe which may be attributed to the laws of association, and are neither more nor less wonderful than the fact that the sun continues to rise.

Imagine a child looking up at a star in the clear night sky. She then shifts her gaze to another star a few degrees away. In reality, those two stars are perhaps uncountable trillions of miles apart, and the light from one will not reach the other for centuries; and yet that child has shifted her attention across the yawning gap from one to the other in the blink of an eye. Similarly, you can in one instant remember something from the past and in the next moment imagine the far future. In these senses at least, consciousness seems to exist outside space and time. If the vitalist has direct knowledge of such abilities within his own mind, can he expect less of what must be a much greater mind-force in the outer world?

Carl Jung, that most mystical of psychologists, used to delight in coincidences. They formed the basis of his famous theory of 'synchronicity', in which he proposed the idea that there must be some kind of 'acausal connecting principle' which links events together. He eventually wrote two books about the theory, one in collaboration with the German physicist Wolfgang Pauli. Here follows an example of a coincidence from his collection.

In the morning of 1 April 1949 Jung copied down a Latin inscription which made reference to fish. He had fish for lunch that day, and at lunch someone mentioned 'April Fish' (a German idiom for 'April Fool'). That afternoon a former patient showed up with several pictures of fish which she had painted. That evening someone showed him some embroidery with 'fish-like sea monsters in it'. The next morning another patient told him a dream about fish. At that time he had been studying the fish in symbolism. He adds in a footnote that when he was writing about all these fish coincidences, he was sitting by a lake. He put down his pen and strolled over to a sea-wall, where he found a large dead fish.

All of these incidents seem to be connected by the Law of Similarity. Fishy things attract fishy things.

Here is another Jungian coincidence-story, which he credits to the writer Wilhelm von Scholz. Before the First World War, a young mother took a picture of her little boy in the Black Forest. She left it in Strassbourg to be developed, but lost track of it when the war broke out. During the war she gave birth to a daughter, and she bought some film in order to take a picture of her daughter.

When the film was developed it was found to be double-exposed: the picture underneath was the photograph she had taken of her son in 1914! The old film had not been developed and had somehow got into circulation again among the new films.[9]

Here the coincidence consisted of the rejoining of the mother with the photographic film, with which she had long been out of contact. There was the further connection of similar circumstances, namely the taking of pictures of her children. Thus both contiguity and similarity seem to have been implicated in this happening.

If the mechanist is hard-pressed to account for such events, the difficulty is directly due to a lack of belief in external mentalism as a regulating principle in nature. The vitalist has no such problem.

As a further corollary of vitalism, a person who believes that the association laws have unconfined validity will probably seek to take advantage of these laws in order to arrange events to his liking, just as he might take advantage of the lever laws of conventional physics to move a rock. It is this impulse to work one's will through the mindlike aspect of the world that is the true origin of magic and sorcery. We will explore this issue in the next chapter.

4. THE NATURE OF RUNE MAGIC

Profit thou hast
  if thou hearest,
Great thy gain
  if thou learnest.
    —Havamal

Rune magic is essentially the magic of words and spells, although it is often combined with other forms of magical symbolism. Word-magic of this sort is very similar to prayer in intent and in function. In both instances, the supplicant invokes some spirit, deity, or unseen power to alter the natural course of events in his behalf, and in either case a sacrifice is often made or promised.

There is a passage in Vigaglum's Saga which relates how a man named Thorkel was compelled to sell his land at Thvera to another man named Glum. Before he left the region, Thorkel led an ox to the temple hallowed to Frey and said the following:

> Frey, who hast for these many years been my guardian, and hast taken many offerings from me and rewarded me well for them, I now bring this ox to thee so that Glum may be driven from the realm of Thvera despite all he can do, just as I go from this land now. Grant me a sign that thou hast heard me and wilt take this gift.

At that moment the ox gave a bellow and slumped down, dead in its tracks. Thorkel took cheer at this, for now he knew Frey had heard his prayer.

The details vary from one locale or time or tribe to another. The gods to whom prayers and offerings are made may have different names and presumed powers. The exact words of the spells and the ingredients of the charms may be as various as the magicians who create them, but aboriginal Australian sorcerers practise rites based upon the same fundamental principles as do American Indian medicine men, tribal African sorcerers, and shamans among the Siberian tribesmen.

No matter where ritual magic is practised nor by whom, at a deep level it is essentially the same around the world. The laws of magic are based on those of mind. The first is that like produces like, or that an effect resembles its cause. This is known as the Law of Similarity. Secondly, things once in contact with one another will retain a mystical linkage and continue to act on each other even after they have become physically separated. This is the law of Contagion. Sir James Frazer noted this many years ago in his famous work, the *Golden Bough*.

> From the first of these principles, namely the Law of Similarity, the magician infers that he can produce any effect he desires merely by imitating it: from the second he infers that whatever he does to a material object will affect equally the person with whom the object was once in contact, whether it formed part of his body or not.[10]

A third law is that magic will be effective in direct proportion to the amount of emotional energy invested by the magician. The Anglo-Polish anthropologist Bronislaw Malinowski wrote of his field studies of magic among the Islanders of the South Pacific, describing a rite in which the sorcerer is trying to kill an enemy with a magical dart:

> If a spectator were suddenly transported to some part of Melanesia and could observe the sorcerer at work, not perhaps knowing exactly what he was looking at, he might think that he had either to do with a lunatic or else he would guess that here was a man acting under the sway of uncontrolled anger. For the sorcerer has, as an essential part of the ritual performance, not merely to point the bone dart at his victim, but with an intense expression of fury and hatred he has to thrust it in the air, turn and twist it as if to bore it in the wound, then pull it back with a sudden jerk. Thus not only is the act of violence, or stabbing, reproduced, but the passion of violence has to be enacted.[11]

Devices such as voodoo dolls employ all of these laws. The doll is made to resemble the intended victim, evoking the principle of Similarity; the victim's hair, fingernails, or clothes will be incorporated into the doll if the magician can lay hands on them, and the evildoer will then mutilate the doll in a highly charged rite infused with strong emotions, thus adding in the effect of the Arousal principle.

Rune magic, just as much as Native American rain dance ceremonies, Melanesian love-magic, or Haitian voodoo rites, is based on these three laws. A given rune acquires its symbolic meaning through *contiguity*, by the arbitrary and repeated pairing of the letter-shape with the idea which it has come to represent. Second, the symbolic values of the runes are linked to events in the real world by virtue of the *similarity* between the symbolism and the reality. And third, the runes are always invoked or activated under the *arousing* circumstances of an emotionally charged consecration ritual, and usually to create magic or to do a reading for a purpose which itself has strong emotional aspects.

In magic, the effectiveness of a tradition is directly related to its antiquity and range. The runes have power because they were long and widely used with defined and relatively invariant meanings. Similarly, the oldest and most widespread forms and meanings of the runes are the ones most richly charged with symbolic connections. For these reasons I believed it important to seek out the deepest roots of the runic oracular and magical traditions.

It is worth noting in passing that Rupert Sheldrake explores the possible existence of biological effects which are essentially similar to these laws of magic in his book *A New Science of Life* (1979). Research stimulated by Sheldrake's work seems to be demonstrating that certain non-local organizing principles, seemingly the same as these association laws, do indeed exist.

There is no fundamental distinction between 'black' and 'white' magic: there are only magical acts for good and for ignoble purposes. The magician who would use his or her knowledge to harm another may well succeed in doing so, but the price is too high for any sane person to want to pay. Be aware that *this is so even if you feel justified in doing ill to another*, for like attracts like. Evil wishes bring a return of evil, and harm directed outwards will come back to you in one form or another. Forgiveness may or may not be divine, but it is the only safe policy for one who dabbles with magic.

The old Teutonic peoples recognized two types of magic, *galdr* and *seid*. *Galdr* was the magic of Odin and of poets. It included rune magic, the casting of spells, and other similar practices. This form of magic was thought to be capable of accomplishing quite deadly results, and was often used for purposes which we would classify as 'black magic', but the pagan Germanic peoples held it to be honourable. *Seid*, at least in some of its forms, on the other hand, was recognized as a thoroughly depraved business. It included sexual perversity and other rites which were too disgusting even for the strong stomachs of these people, who routinely practised several very bloody forms of human sacrifice as well as necromancy (i.e. magic which makes use of human corpses).

The runemasters of northern Europe left behind many examples of their magical art. For the most part, these took the form of blessings and curses placed on various appropriate objects. One monument stone has carved on it the words: 'Prophecy of danger! Runes of honour I now conceal here, runes of power. Pursued by perversity, exposed to a miserable death, will he be who destroys this (monument).'

Scholars now think that many apparent 'mistakes' made by the rune carvers of old were done deliberately in order to satisfy numerological formulas. People familiar with one or another system of numerology might want to try their hands at using the traditional runic number system to create runic messages which add up to meaningful values.

The traditional rune-magicians divided the Futhark into three 'families', or *aettir*, each of which contained eight characters. In this system each rune had a family number and a position number within its row, the rows being numbered conventionally as in column A below or in later years sometimes from bottom to top, as in Column B:

A	B	1	2	3	4	5	6	7	8
1	3	ᚠ	ᚢ	ᚦ	ᚨ	ᚱ	ᚲ	ᚷ	ᚹ
2	2	ᚺ	ᚾ	ᛁ	ᛃ	ᛇ	ᛈ	ᛉ	ᛊ
3	1	ᛏ	ᛒ	ᛖ	ᛗ	ᛚ	ᛜ	ᛞ	ᛟ

Modern numerologists usually work with the position numbers only, ignoring the family numbers. There is evidence that the old Germanic spell-makers frequently did the same. There are also instances in which they used the 'whole numbers'

Figure 11: Golden bracteate found at Vadstena, Sweden.

of the runes, from 1 for FEHU to 24 for ODALA.

One of the most widespread rune charms among the ancients was the Futhark itself. Rune-rows were carved on bones and grave monuments and tree roots, concealed in buildings, buried in tombs, placed almost anywhere that an enemy wouldn't find them. Any charm gains its power by the special magical arrangement of its elements; the Futhark contains the rune symbols in their 'resting' positions, and is therefore employed to 'defuse' the malign rune-spells of others by putting the elements back safely into their normal order.

A talisman found in Sweden and reliably dated to about AD 525 is worth special attention here because it so neatly illustrates several principles of rune magic. The talisman is a finely worked, coin-shaped neck pendant made of gold. In the centre are depicted a stylized head (human or god), a bird (likely an eagle), and an animal, probably a horse. Around the outside of the picture is a runic inscription which consists of the characters ᚠᚢᚹᚱᛏᚢᛈᚠ plus the Futhark divided into the *aettir*, thus:

ᚠᚢᚦᚨᚱᚲᚷᚹ:ᚺᚾᛁᛃᛇᛈᛉᛊ:ᛏᛒᛖᛗᛚᛜᛟᛞ *

---

* The D- and O-runes were reversed from their normal positions at the end of the rune-row. Several other examples of rune-rows with this reversal have been found, indicating that it was a variant ordering rather than just an error in the making of the medallion. This book follows the apparent 'majority opinion' of antiquity in giving the D-O ending as standard.

By separating the rune-row into the *aettir*, the maker of the charm clearly indicated knowledge of, and concern with, the number values of the characters.

The word 'LUWATUWA' has no known meaning. However, when it is divided into its two obvious halves and position numbers are assigned to the runes, here is what results:

ᛚ ᚢ ᚹ ᚨ   ᛏ ᚢ ᚹ ᚨ
5 2 3 4   1 2 3 4

I believe that the first word is intended to communicate the state of something being out of order, just as the numbers 5-2-3-4 are out of sequence. To correct this sequence the first character is changed: the rune for healing is replaced with that for victory. This transformation is accomplished by the minimal step of adding a small diagonal line to the left top of the LAUKZ rune. The second word, which results from this alteration, has two distinguishing characteristics: the number sequence is normalized (1-2-3-4), and the word begins and ends with a god-rune. To my eye, the two words (or word-halves) plus the Futhark are an ingeniously conceived, very compact spell to be read as follows: 'May healing succeed. May there be victory, strength, joy, and wisdom, under the protection of the gods. May everything be put to rights, and may all harmful spells be dissipated.'

For a touch of added symbolism, the inscription was magically bound into itself in a ring around the edge of the coin, thus surrounding the depicted person, bird, and animal protectively. The bird probably symbolized Odin in his aspect of the god of magic and wisdom. Rings had a special significance among these people as symbols of loyalty. Vikings swore oaths on a ring mounted on the door of the pagan temple, and the Ring-Danes in *Beowulf* were so-named because they wore arm bracelets as tokens of their loyalty to the local king.

What a genius the maker of this amulet was, to code so much into so few characters, taking full advantage of numerology, the meanings of the individual runes, and the concept of the Futhark as a symbol for countering evil spells.

You can make use of this symbolism to create your own protective charms: just inscribe the runic alphabet in its correct order on a long strip of wood or paper, or around the cir-

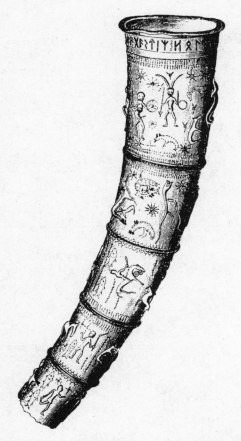

Figure 12: Drawing of a golden drinking horn found at Gallehus, Jùtland, dating from around AD 500. The original is no longer in existance, having been stolen and melted down (*from Stephens, 1884, p.87*).

cumference of a ring shape of your own making. Such objects can be placed at the entrances of your home, in your car, or in your workplace to symbolically disarm harmful thoughts and energies.

The runes were also commonly used as ingredients in the magical potions served to heroes in the legends, and perhaps in reality, to give them magical powers. Here is how one legendary warrior described the recipe for a drink the Valkyrie Grimhild gave to him:

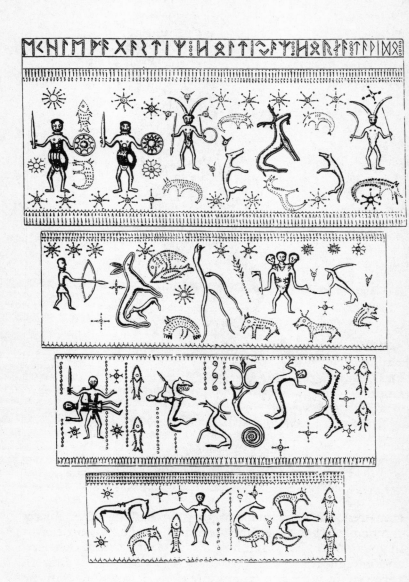

Figure 13

Then Grimhild handed me
  a full horn to drink,
    cool and bitter,
      that cast out grief;
In it was mixed
  the might of Earth,
    the ice-cold sea,
      and the blood of swine.
Carved on the horn
  were many runes
    painted red——
      I could not read them——
A long serpent
  out of the sea,
    an ear of corn,
      entrails of beasts.
Baleful things
  were mixed in that beer,
    herbs from the forest,
      fireblackened acorns,
The hearth's dew, soot,
  entrails of sacrifices,
    boiled swine's liver,
      soothing to sorrow.

It would take a hero to drink it. If any reader decides to try this recipe—perhaps as a remedy for a hangover—I believe I would prefer not to know anything about the undertaking.

You can make a simpler and far more hygienic magic rune potion by writing a runic blessing with red food colouring on some safe piece of wood such as a new tongue depressor and consecrating the runes with the coin ceremony described in the next section. Then stir the stick in a glass of beer or tea until the message dissolves into the beverage and drink it.

Whether carving a talismanic blessing or charging a drink with rune power, you can employ the runes in either of two ways: you can simply use the runes to write your message phonetically in English (using the phonetic table given in the appendix) or you can select individual runes on the basis of their symbolic or numerological values and string them together into a charm. The most potent magic will result from taking all these various values into consideration, as did the maker of the talisman described above. You might even ask the runes to arrange themselves into a meaningful triplet for some specific purposes by drawing three as if you were doing a reading.

Runes were written either from left to right or right to left, sometimes in alternating directions from one row to another, and individual letters, particularly ᚼ, ⟨ and ᛋ, might vary in the direction they faced, right or left, within the same line or even the same word. A clever rune worker could sometimes turn this lack of standardization to his advantage. One of the earliest known rune stones in Sweden has on it the magical word ᚼᚾᛘᚾᚼ. We note that this word is a palindrome—one can read it from left to right or vice versa—and furthermore, the beginning and final ᚼ-runes are mirror images, thus reinforcing the idea of reversibility.

RUNE SPELLS

You don't need to learn the old Germanic tongue in order to do rune magic; however, the ancient rune masters made extensive use of certain stock phrases, usually only two words long and of a certain characteristic form, in their magical work and you can easily incorporate some of these original elements in your own spells. For example, GIBU AUJA (ᚷᛁᛒᚢ : ᚠᚢᛉᚨ) means 'I give prosperity'. It is one of the all-time most popular Runic messages of ancient times, having been carved on rock slabs and boulders all across Scandinavia.

You have undoubtedly noticed that GIBU (ᚷᛁᛒᚢ) means 'I give' or 'I bring' (note that the related rune name GEBU is the noun which means 'gift'). Likewise, LAThU (ᛚᚨᚦᚢ) means 'I invite' or 'I summon'.

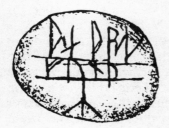

Figure 14: Stephens, a nineteenth-century rune scholar, believed this south inscribed store was an amulet for finding a thief. He reads the inscription as *Thiwbio Funthr*, 'Thief-find', and comments that it was used with water and a small mirror to reveal the image of the criminal. Dated about AD 750-800 from Frederiksberg, Sealand, Denmark, it measures roughly an inch across (*from Stephen, 1885: p.98*)

For variety, you can use either of these words in combination with any of the following nouns to make your own authentic runic spells in the old language:

Old Germanic	Modern English
ᚠᚢᛉᚨ AUJA	Prosperity, increase
ᚼᛁᚷ SIG	Victory
ᚠᛚᚢᚷᛟᛗ ALUGOD	Good magic
ᚨᚢᛈᚱ AUDR	Wealth
ᚡᚱᚠᛗᛁ FRAMI	Fame

Thus 'GIBU SIG' (ᚷᛁᛒᚢ : ᚼᛁᚷ) means 'I give (or bring) victory' and 'LAThU ALUGOD' (ᛚᚨᚦᚢ : ᚠᛚᚢᚷᛟᛗ) translates as 'I summon Good Magic'. You can also use LAThU or GIBU with any apporpriate rune names; thus GIBU WUNJU is 'I give Joy', LAThU JARA means 'I invite a bountiful year', etc.

BIND RUNES

It was a common practice for rune magicians to combine two or more runes together into a single character, called a 'bind-rune'. This was done for any of several reasons. Sometimes a troublesome letter had to be disposed of in order to satisfy a numerological formula. In other cases the bind-rune was simply an abbreviation for a common word or phrase. For example bind-runes 1 and 2 below are composed of the characters G and A (or A and G). The ambiguity of the order allows them to simultaneously represent GIBU AUJA and ALU GOD.

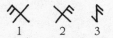

In a number of cases the intent was to mystify the uninitiated. Bind-rune 3 above, which has been found carved, sometimes alone and sometimes as part of longer messages, on stones around in northern Europe, illustrates several of these principles at once. The single stave has two branches to the right on top, yielding the A-rune while the branch pointing left from the bottom of the stave forms an inverted LAUKZ (ᚴ). These two characters are not hard to see—but when the figure is read as a secret rune (see page 88) a third letter can be found, identified by its Aett (family) and position number. One branch to the right means First Aett; two branches to the left means Second Position. The rune with this value (assuming that the Aettir are numbered as in Figure 1, Column A above) is URUZ. This remarkable triple bind-rune therefore spells a-l-u: *Alu*: a word which is known only from rune carvings, and which means (protective) Magic.

Although this word is attested only on runic inscriptions, it is related to the Old Norse/Icelandic word *ala*, which means 'to give birth to, to nurture,' Another related usage is Ol in the expression 'Ol-runes', usually translated 'ale runes', which occurs frequently in the poems of the Elder Edda. The past tense (singular) of *ala* is *ol*, so perhaps a pun is intended here—a way of intensifying the meaning of a given word. Puns are considered to have magical significance, so they are very often found in runic inscriptions.

RULES FOR WRITING SPELLS

Certain is that
  which is sought from runes,
That the gods so great have
made
  and the *erilaZ* painted...

Runes shalt thou find,   .
  and fateful signs
That the king of singers coloured
  and the mighty gods have
made;
Full strong the signs,
  full mighty the signs
That the ruler of gods doth write. ·
—Havamal

The word *erilaZ* (ᛗᚱᛁᛚᚨᛉ) is usually translated 'rune-master' and carries with it the added meanings of 'poet' and 'sorcerer'. Since large numbers of their rune inscriptions have been found—including some which they had hidden in graves and bogs and in other places which they hoped would never again see the light of day—we can study the work they left behind them and discover some of the rules and principles which guided them in creating spells.

Figure 15: 'Thorfastr made a good comb.' Inscribed Viking comb case found in Lincolnshire, England, is shown with a comb which, though it comes from Sealand in Denmark, must be very much like the one which was hinged into the Lincolnshire case.

Consider the following two translations from runic inscriptions:

'Thorfstr made a good comb.'

'Halfdan Geirsson is the best erilaЗ in Trondheim.'

The first text was incised on a bone comb found in Lincolnshire (see Figure 4); the second is of a form which might be found hidden in swamps, in lakes, or offshore in the sea anywhere in the Germanic realms, with only the personal and place names changing to suit the occasion.

Some modern runologists are reluctant to concede magical purposes for rune inscriptions. They tend to see messages like these as simple boasts or as some sort of primitive public relations efforts.

But don't Thorfastr's runes seem rather pointless if this is all he had in mind? And inscriptions of the sort Halfdan made would have been doubly purposeless because the writers generally went to great trouble to *conceal* their messages from the prying eyes of others.

I find it far more likely that Thorfastr carved the runes *before* he made the comb, and that he did so as a precautionary magical act to ensure that nothing would go wrong in the process of making the comb—none of its teeth breaking off as he shaped them, for instance.

Similarly those who, like Halfdan, made and hid runic declarations that they were the best at something, or that some desired state had come to pass, were not primarily or necessarily asserting the truth of their statements; rather, they were creating spells which they hoped would bring about or maintain the specified conditions. It would then certainly make sense for them to hide their rune spells so that potential rivals or enemies cannot undo them.

Figure 16: The Jarsberg Stone from Varnum, Vermland, Sweden, dating from about AD 500 (*from Stephens, 1884; p.29*)

Knowest how to write them,
  knowest how to advise?
Knowest how to paint them,
  knowest how one makes trial?
Knowest how to ask them,
  knowest how one shall offer?
Knowest how to send to them,
  knowest how to sacrifice?
                        —Havamal

Both Halfdan's and Thorfastr's spells follow a standard formula, just as if they had both been consulting the same Handbook of Applied Rune Magic. Here are some of the rules which that hypothetical manual might have contained:

1 Do not hesitate to identify yourself. This will ensure that the gods know whom they are supposed to be helping. One old-time rune worker identified himself by both name and nickname: 'I, the ErilaZ, am named UbaZ. I am called HarabanaZ (Raven). I carve runes' (Figure 5).

Many runestones intended as grave memorials name the dead man, the relatives who commissioned the stone, and the *erilaZ* who carved it and usually contain a spell which threatens terrible consequences for anyone who dares disturb the burial site. The following text, carved on a stone at Glavendrup, Denmark in about AD 900-925 is a good example:

> Ragnild raised this stone in memory of Alli, *Godi* (pagan priest) in Salve, revered chief of the temple. Alli's sons raised this monument in memory of their father, and his wife for her husband, while Soti carved these runes for his master. May Thor hallow these runes. May he pay most hideously for his crime whoever dares overturn this stone or remove it from this place.

Sometimes the *erilaZ* displayed his skaldic skill by putting the text of the inscription into verse:

Aesbaern hewed the stone,
  stained in memory,
    bound with runes;
Gylla raised it
  after Gairbern,
    her husband,
And Gudfrid
  after her father.

He was best
  of the dwellers in Kil.
Let him read who can.

In some instances the *erilaZ* chose to conceal his name lest others find his runework and be able to turn it on him. He might then identify himself in some fashion which the gods would understand but other mortals would not. Perhaps this explains the following inscription, found at Maeshowe, Orkney:

> These runes were cut by that man who is most skilled in runes west over the sea, with that axe which Gauk, Trandil's son, in the south (of Iceland) owned.

2 State the desired end as if it were an accomplished fact: 'I *am* the best. . ., not 'I wish to become. . .'; likewise, 'Thorfastr *made* a good comb', not 'Thorfastr hopes this comb doesn't break while he's working on it'. Think about it: like attracts like, and unfulfilled wishes are not what you wish to attract.

3 Don't demand more than you need. Halfdan was only staking out the city of Trondheim; he didn't hope to become the best *erilaZ* in all the world, or even all of Norway. Likewise, Thorfastr was willing to settle for a *good* comb.

4 Rune spells and charms should be dedicated, or 'charged', with a sacrifice of some sort. The word for sacrifice is blott, etymologically from the same root as blød, 'blood'. Often sheep, goats, cattle, and sometimes even people, were offered up to the gods in olden times. Recall how in Grettis Saga the old sorceress cuts herself and uses her own blood to activate a murderous rune curse. But in today's circumstances there is little opportunity, need, or justification for killing some hapless animal or giving up your own blood in order to do rune magic. Some modern Odinists bake large animal-shaped biscuits to use as effigies in their rituals.

There is also a coin-sacrifice rite for consecrating wooden rune pieces for use in divination, described in the next chapter. If you wish, you can modify this ceremony for use in spell-magic. Just change the incantation as appropriate and make the coin offering as usual. If you have made a charm which says 'I bring prosperity' ask Odin (or, if you wish, the Powers of Good) to take note of what you ask and then say 'These runes have started money on its way to me' nine times while surrendering nine coins one by one to the lake.

These days, since virtually nobody knows how to read runes, you can most likely even leave your rune charms safely out in plain sight, or you can go through the old rites of burning or hiding them if you wish.

5 'Knowest how to colour them?' The paint has weathered off most of the stones by now, but we know that runic carvings, particularly those created for magical purposes, were often painted red to symbolize blood. Alternatively, if made on wood, the letters might be branded in to symbolize the holy flames which were kept burning in some of the temples. Letters charred into wood also have a symbolic connection to the ancient Germanic fire rites which were used for several magical purposes as in the custom of offering up of rune messages and sacrifices by burning them, driving evil spirits or spells from newly claimed territory by carrying flames around the fields, etc.

6 When a rune-master wished to invoke the literal meaning of a rune, he commonly repeated it three times. These lines from the *Skirnismal* tell of how Skirnir, the servant of Frey, put a spell on a giant-maiden:

> Thrice ThurisaƵ I write
>   and mark thee therewith:
> Longing and madness and lust.
>
> But the signs I have made
>   I may yet unwrite
> If I find a cause therefore.

ThurisaƵ is the rune which stands for 'giant' or 'ogre'. The irony of bewitching a giant-maid with the giant's rune was of course deliberate.

The so-called Gummarp stone (now unfortunately lost) bore an inscription which translates as: 'Hathuwolf set down these runestaves: ᚠ ᚠ ᚠ ' (cattle, property, wealth). In the same vicinity was found another stone which reads 'The new farm tenants gave Hathuwolf ᚾᚾᚾ' (a prosperous year, a fertile season, a bountiful period). Most runologists read the second stone literally, and Krause remarks on how it seems to be an answer to the first. I suspect, however, that it was simply an amplification of the desire for prosperity which had motivated the making of the first stone, the desired outcome being expressed in the past tense as per Rule 2 above. The GEBU rune was also frequently tripled in prosperity charms, especially in the form of the *Gibu Auja/Alu God* bind-runes (ᚷ, ᛉ) discussed above.

Figure 17: The Franks Casket (*from Stephens, 1884: pp 144-5*).

The Franks Casket (Figure 17) is a small whalebone box made in Northumbria in about AD700 which makes repeated use of trebled-rune formulas to invoke the magical values of the rune names. Named for A.W. Franks, who found it in France and donated it to the British Museum, the casket measures 9 × 7.5 × 4.25 inches and is decorated with elaborate carvings surrounded by inscriptions in the English runes. According to an analysis by the German runologist Alfred Becker, both the pictures and the inscriptions were done with the intention of creating magic to protect the contents of the box and to increase the wealth of the owner. The inscriptions consist of poetry carefully constructed so that the first rune of each of three pairs of syllables, F (*fehu*—cattle, possession, money), and G (*gebu*—gift), appears three times in alternation as a formula to conjure wealth. Other magical purposes are sought through the trebled use of the R- and T-runes, indicating 'ride, travel' and 'victory and justice', respectively.

A small medallion found at Skodbog in south Jutland bears a much simpler text, which also illustrates the principle of tripling. Transliterated and separated into words, it reads 'auja alawin auja alawin auja alawin j alawid: 'Prosperity to Alvin; Prosperity to Alvin; Prosperity to Alvin; j (a good harvest) to Alvin'.

MAGIC FOR YOUR IMPLEMENTS

The ancient warriors went into combat with rune charms on their broadswords, axes, and spear heads. The Valkyrie

Figure 18: Pre-Viking Swedish spear found in Russia. The inscription reads *Tilarings*, perhaps the owner's name *(from Stephens, 1884; p.204)*.

Sigrdrifa ('Victory-Bringer') tells the hero Sigure (whom Wagner called Siegfried in his operas):

> Victory-runes learn
> if thou seekest to win
> And the runes
> On thy sword-hilt scratch;
> Some in the blade-groove
> And some on the flat
> And twice call on TiwaZ.

We seldom carry spears or swords any more, so this bit of rune lore may at first thought seem to be of limited use. But think again. The general principle involved is that putting the proper runes on an object will give it magical assistance in fulfilling its purpose. If you play tennis (and your name is Jane) you can inscribe your racquet with the message 'This racquet brings victory to Jane' or in runes:

ᚦᛇᛋ:ᚱᚨᛇᚲᛖᛏ:ᛒᚱᛇᚾᚷᛉ:ᚢᛇᚲᛏᛖᚱᛁ:ᛏᚢᚹ:ᛃᛖᛇᚾ

A woodworker might engrave on the side of his carpenter's pencil:

ᛃᚨᚾ:ᛗᚨᚱᚲᛋ:ᛏᚱᚢᚹ:ᚹᛇᚦ:ᛗᛁ

('John marks true with me').

For a golfer,

ᚦᛇᛋ:ᛈᚢᛏᛇᚱ:ᛋᚺᚢᚹᛏᛋ:ᛋᛏᚱᛖᛁᛏ

('This putter shoots straight').

Don't overlook the possibilities of safety magic. Since we use axes somewhat differently now than they did in the old days, you might employ an electric engraving tool to put the following runes on the head of your axe:

ᚦᛇᛋ:ᚨᛇᚲᛋ:ᛋᛈᛚᛇᛏᛋ:ᚹᚢᛞ:ᚾᛟᛏ:ᚠᛚᛇᛋᚺ

('This axe splits wood, not flesh').

Also for your car,

ᚦᛇᛋ:ᚱ:ᛏᚱᚨᛇᚠᛚᛉ:ᛇᚠᛇᚱ:ᛇᚾ:ᛋᛖᛁᚠᛏᛁ

('This "chariot" travels ever in safety').

If you set your imagination free you will discover many more applications for simple rune magic of this sort. Write a charm

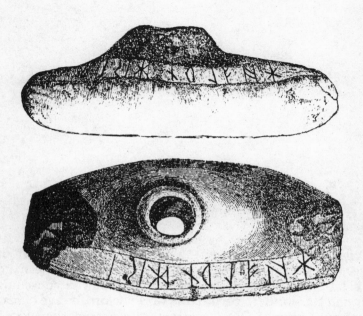

Figure 19: 'Oltha owns this axe' This inscription may have been intended as a magical as a mundane aid to Oltha (a woman) in retaining possession of her stone axe. Dated about AD 600-700, Upsala, Upland, Sweden (*from Stephens, 1884; p. 78*).

for your bicycle to prevent its being stolen: 'The thief's mind goes blank when he sees this bike'; make a safety-spell for your lawnmower, perhaps etching onto its blade a protective device like that for the axe above; write protection charms for the entrances of your house: 'This door opens only to those of good will'). As with all rune magic, you should *magna* (consecrate) your inscriptions with the coin sacrifice ritual.

5. RUNES IN THE SAGAS

'Sagen, singen, und trinken': tale-telling, singing, and carousing. The German phrase concisely summarizes the major recreations available in the long, snowbound winter evenings around the northern parts of the world before the age of mass communications. The Germanic folk passed the gloomy months of isolation with traditional tales of gods and heroes, of tribal history and fantasy. Stories and poems were passed down from age to age, subjected to the vagaries of human memory, to the creative alterations of succeeding generations of storytellers, and finally to the ideological demands of Christianity after the new religion arrived on the scene.

There were the long, rambling poems which were collected together into the Poetic Edda, or Elder Edda. Some of these poems told how the world was created from the body of a giant and prophesied how it would end in a great battle between the gods and the forces of Chaos. Some recounted the doings of the gods, or gave sage advice on how to conduct oneself in life. Others recounted the great deeds of men such as Atli, known to the rest of the world as Attila the Hun, and Sigurd/Siegfried, around whom Wagner created his famous operatic cycle. Most of the verses quoted in this book come from the Poetic Edda.

The Younger Edda is a prose work by a remarkable thirteenth-century Icelandic scholar and politician named Snorri Sturluson. In it he wrote down all the stories he could collect about the old religion and related topics. He presented this pagan material with the excuse that it was a work for 'young poets who want to study poetic diction and enrich their style with ancient designations or who wish to understand the hidden meaning of poetry', thus placing his book in a context acceptable to the early Icelandic Christian establishment. The saving of this information, much of which we have from no other sources, is only one of the literary deeds for which posterity owes Snorri a debt of gratitude. He also wrote two historical works, the *Heimskringla* and St. Olaf's Saga, based on materials he collected on a trip to Norway and Sweden, and is generally thought to be the author of Egil's Saga, which we will shortly examine.

The Sagas were long prose histories and romances, each of which would take several evenings in the telling. Thus they were ideal for helping to while away the many nights between the first deep snows of winter and the return of the sun in spring. Some of the sagas were frankly fictional, while others were based on real people and events. Scholars of the last century or so have made careers of sorting out the historical from the apocryphal material in these stories. In many instances, the sagas represent actual historical happenings about as well as old dime Western novels tell the true story of the American frontier: that is, there is often a core of truth in there somewhere under all the distortions and embellishments. But regardless of their absolute historicity, there is no denying that these stories have much to tell us about the ideas, concerns, and beliefs of the people who told them.

Still, there was plenty of time and opportunity for inaccuracies to occur, for it was not until the thirteenth century, and then only in Iceland, that remote western outpost of the nordic world where the old ways and the old language never really died, that anyone began committing the oral literature of the Eddas and the sagas to paper.

Two of the sagas contain stories of special relevance to students of the runic tradition. The first of these, and perhaps the most famous of all, is Egil's Saga.

INCIDENTS FROM EGIL'S SAGA

Egil Skallagrimsson was a pagan Icelandic warrior and poet whose life nearly spanned the tenth century. The saga which

bears his name tells the deeds of his family for four generations, beginning with his immediate ancestors and how they
came to leave Norway. The portion of the story which deals
with Egil himself deals mostly with his three major excur-
sions out from Iceland and his running feud with Eirik
Bloody-Axe, a petty Norwegian king, and his queen Gunnhild.

Egil was precocious at two skills much prized by the Vikings: poetry and bloodletting. To call him headstrong would
be to indulge in hopeless understatement. When he was seven
years old he was playing a ball game with an older and
stronger child. The other child, named Grim, made the mistake of pushing Egil too hard in the game. Egil flew into a
rage and hit Grim with a bat. The older boy then lay hands
on Egil and gave him a beating, forcing Egil to slink off smart-
ing under the jeers of the other children as much as from
his bruises. Egil returned to the playing field with an axe and
buried it in Grim's head. This killing inspired a battle among
the adults in which seven died.

Egil apparently came by his murderous tendencies naturally. When he was twelve he got involved in another multi-
ple killing over a ball game. He and a friend were playing ball
against his father. When Egil's side began to win, his father
started the violence by picking up Egil's teammate and dash-
ing him to death on the ground. Then he went for Egil but
a servant woman who had fostered the boy intervened, saying 'Do you now go berserk against your own son, Skallagrim?' At this, Skallagrim chased her until she jumped off
a cliff into the sea and then hit her with a rock so that she
drowned. Egil retaliated against his father by murdering his
father's foreman. It was observed that neither Egil nor his
father ever spoke of this incident afterwards.

The next spring Egil wanted to sail to Norway with his older
brother Thorolf, but Thorolf did not want to take him, saying 'If your father cannot manage you here at home, I cannot risk having you aboard my ship, for your vile temper could
be the end of us all'.

'Then perhaps we shall both stay here', said Egil. The next
night there was a storm and he cut his brother's ship free
from its moorings so that it was blown out to sea, finally coming to rest on the shore of an island to the southwest. Egil
insisted that he would continue to do mischief to his brother

until he was allowed to go along. Thorolf's crew intervened between the brothers and Egil was finally permitted to go along.

In their travels, Thorolf and Egil came to an island where King Eirik, who ruled a region in Norway, had a big house which he left in the charge of a man named Bard. The brothers and their party were wet and tired from travelling in foul weather and so asked Bard for a night's lodging. Bard agreed, but set them a scanty table and gave them no ale, saying he had none.

That very evening the king and his wife Gunnhild arrived for a feast and *disablot* rite. The king invited the brothers and their crew to join his party, so they got the ale and sumptious food they had earlier been denied. Egil got very drunk and made up a poem which insulted Bard for his earlier stinginess. Bard kept pushing more drink on Egil and then went to complain about him to Queen Gunnhild. She and Bard mixed a poison into a horn of ale and brought it to Egil, thinking to settle his insolence permanently. But Egil pulled a knife from his belt and cut himself in the palm. Then he took hold of the horn, carved some runes around its lip, and smeared the letters with his own blood. He sang:

> Carve we runes on horn now,
> With red blood make words ruddy;
> Here are the words I'm wanting
> On tree of aurochs ear-root*:
> Drain we what drink we crave for
> When merry maidens pour;
> Learn if fares foul or fairly
> The ale this Bard has hallowed.

*'Tree of aurochs ear-root' is a kenning (i.e. a poetic phrase) for a drinking-horn.

The horn ruptured from the magic of the runes and words, and the drink spilled harmlessly to the floor. Egil then snatched a full horn away from one of his party who had had too much. Downing this at one long pull, he tossed the empty horn over his shoulder, drew his sword, and plunged it through Bard. Then he ran out into the night.

Though the king's men hunted him for all night, Egil got away by swimming to a nearby island. There he hid until his searchers gave up and he could rejoin his brother and continue the journey.

Many years later Egil again had a run-in with King Eirik, this time in a legal dispute over an inheritance. Eirik ended up declaring Egil an outlaw and once more set his men out to hunt him. Egil once more killed some of his pursuers and eluded the rest, setting up a scorn-pole against Eirik and robbing a farm as he went.

The scorn-pole was made of hazel wood, which was known for its magic properties. Egil set the pole up on a rocky promontory with a mare's head on top to signify that Eirik was 'mare-hearted', or cowardly. Then he recited a spell:

> I here set up a scorn-pole, and I place this scorn on the king and his queen. I aim this scorn at the spirits who inhabit this land (Landvaet-tir), that they may all become lost and not find their way back until the king and his wife be driven from their realm.

Then he carved this spell on the pole in runes and left. Whether one wishes to attribute it to Egil's scorn-pole or not, Eirik and Gunnhild were eventually driven from Norway.

It was on another journey some years later that the last significant rune story occurs in Egil's Saga. Egil was travelling with a band of men in what is now the Swedish province of Värmland and he stopped at the farm of a man named Thorfinn to take breakfast and feed the horses.

As they were eating, Egil saw that there was a sick woman lying in the sleeping area of the farmer's hall. He asked who she was. Thorfinn told him she was his daughter Helga, and her strength had been sinking for some time. She was unable to sleep and had been delirious at times.

'What have you done for her?' asked Egil.

'Runes have been made for her. My neighbour's son carved them, but it did not help. She has gotten worse than before,' replied the farmer. 'Do you know how to cure this dreadful wasting away?'

'I suppose I can hardly make things worse for her,' said Egil. 'Let me have a try.' So he went to where she was lying and spoke with her. He instructed the others to lift her up from where she lay, replace her bedclothes with clean ones, and air out the ones she had been lying in. They complied. He then searched through the bed where she had been resting. In the mattress straw he found a piece of whalebone with runes carved on it. He read the runes, shaved them off into the fire with his knife, and burned the rest of the bone. Then he sang:

No leech* should turn loose runes
Except he can read them well;
It is so with many a man
That the dark letters bewilder him.
I spied on whittled whalebone
Ten secret rune-staves graven
That have caused to leek-linden
A sorrow all too lasting.

*'Leech' means healer; 'leek-linden' is a kenning for maiden.

Egil completed his medicine by carving healing runes of his own which he put under the girl's pillow. Almost immediately she began to revive, saying that she felt as if she were arising from a long sleep. She said she felt well again, although she had not yet regained back her strength.

As for Egil and his men, the next day it was back to business as usual: eluding the ambushes of his enemies, killing those he could not elude, and extorting wealth from the landowners whose holdings lay in his path.

INCIDENTS FROM GRETTI'S SAGA

Gretti the Strong was a famous Icelandic outlaw who had been banished for murder. He had many noteworthy adventures during the years he lived outside the law, including a hand-to-hand battle with the very physical ghost of a dead thrall (slave) named Glam. He subdued the ghost, decapitated it with his sword and had its body burnt before he could be sure it was done for. There is, however, nothing stranger in Gretti's tale than the story of how he met his death.

Among the many enemies Gretti had made was one called Thorbjorn Angle. Thorbjorn had tried in many ways, both fair and foul, to get rid of Gretti but he could find no plan that would work. Finally he turned to his aged foster-mother Thurid.

She had been a skilled sorceress in her youth, when the people of Iceland were still pagan. By the time of the story, the church had by no means eliminated all traces of heathendom. Many Icelanders still clung to the old ways, conducting their pagan rites in private. The authorities turned a blind eye to all but the most public of heathen practices; only those who were too careless or open were ever sentenced to the three years' banishment which was theoretically prescribed for such doings.

Gretti was by this time barricaded with some friends on the island of Drangey. Thurid made Thorbjorn take her to the island so she could study the situation. In an encounter with Gretti's group, Thurid cursed him from her position in the stern of her son's boat: 'I say this of you, Gretti, that you must lose your health, your luck, and your fortune, and be deprived of friendship, protection, and counsel, the more so the longer you live. I wish each day of your future may be darker than the one before.'

Gretti made reply by throwing a rock at her, and was gratified to hear her scream, for his throw was good and the rock broke her thigh. Thorbjorn and his company withdrew from Drangey. On the way home Thurid swore, 'This is the beginning of Gretti's end. I care not whether or not I live, but he shall sink from this day forward and I shall have my revenge'.

Late summer changed to autumn and winter was pressing down when Thurid, her leg finally healed, demanded to be taken to the sea-shore. 'What do you wish to do?' asked Thorbjorn.

'A trifle only, yet maybe a sign of greater things to come.'

The old woman limped along the strand until she found a great piece of driftwood, a snag of a tree with its roots still attached. She made Thorbjorn turn the stump over until she found a smooth place on the tap root. There she had him make a flat surface with his axe so she could carve runes onto the wood. She cut her finger with her knife, smeared her blood into the rune incisions and mumbled some spells over them. Next she walked backwards widdershins (counterclockwise) around the stump, chanting words of potent evil all the while. After that she told her son to push the piece of driftwood into the fjord.

She commanded it to go to Drangey and do grave harm to Gretti. When Thorbjorn said he did not know what would come of all this, she told him that he would surely find out in the future. The enchanted stump drifted out at a fair speed, and was moving up the fjord *against the wind* when the crone turned her back upon it to go home.

Some days later Thurid's snag had drifted up on the beach at Drangey. Gretti's thrall found it there while searching for firewood in a miserable rain and dragged it into their hut. Gretti picked up his axe and brought it around in a great two-handed swing to split the driftwood, but he landed a glancing blow so that the axe head rebounded off the rune-bewitched wood and sank into his right leg.

Thurid urged Thorbjorn to go to Drangey, and was finally able to convince him that something might have come of her magic. He raised a crew of warriors and set out for his enemy's stronghold.

Gretti's wound never healed properly; instead, it putrefied and he was nearly dead when Thorbjorn arrived. Even so, Thurid's stepson had trouble dispatching the old outlaw, and nicked his sword badly while beheading him.

His murderous deed done, Thorbjorn decided it would be wise to get very far away from Drangey for a while because Gretti had many friends and relatives who were anxious to avenge his death. Thorbjorn sailed for the Mediterranean. In those days Scandinavians were in much demand as warriors in those realms, and he had no trouble securing employment in the Imperial Guards in Constantinople. Unfortunately for him, Gretti's brother Thorsteinn soon found out where he had gone and followed him, even joining the Byzantine Emperor's Varangian (i.e. Scandinavian) Guards to continue his search. Neither knew the other, but one day while the guardsmen were on review Thorbjorn boasted in front of Thorsteinn about having killed Gretti, showing off the nick in his sword. Pretending adulation, Thorsteinn asked to see the sword and the other handed it over. As soon as he had it, Thorsteinn used the sword to kill its owner and thus avenge his brother's death.

6. INDIRECT LANGUAGE AND CONCEALED MEANINGS IN WORD MAGIC AND POETRY

Both for stylistic purposes in poetry and as an integral part of magic, the ancient ones often found it desirable to couch their messages in other than literal terms. In this Prose Edda Snorri devotes an entire section, called 'Poetic Diction', to elaborating on the meanings of the metaphorical phrases and expressions used by the Skaldic poets. He presents the various metaphors, or 'kennings,' in question-and-answer form. The discussion is between a man named Aegir and the god Bragi, who (like Odin and Tyr) is famed for his skill in speech. One passage from this text will serve to give the flavour of the whole.

Aegir asked: 'Where did the accomplishment known as poetry come from?'

Bragi answered:

> The beginning of it was that the gods known as the Aesir were at war with the ones known as the Vanir and they arranged for a peace-meeting between them and made a truce in this way: they both went up to a crock and spat into it. When they were going away, the gods took the truce-token and would not allow it to be lost, and made of it a man. he was called Kvasir. He is so wise that nobody asks him any question that he is unable to answer. He travelled far and wide over the world to teach men wisdom and came once to feast with some dwarfs, Fjalar and Galar. These called him aside for a word in private and killed him, letting his blood run into two crocks and one kettle. The kettle was called Odrörir, but the crocks were known as Son and Bodn. They mixed his blood with honey, and it became the mead which makes

whoever drinks of it a poet or scholar. The dwarfs told the Aesir that Kvasir had choked with learning, because there was no one sufficiently well-informed to compete with him in knowledge.

Then the dwarfs invited a giant called Gilling to their home with his wife, and they asked him to go out rowing on the sea with them. When they were far out, however, the dwarfs rowed on to a rock and upset the boat. Gilling could not swim and was drowned, but the dwarfs righted their craft and rowed ashore. They told his wife about this accident and she was very distressed and wept aloud. Fjalar asked her if she would be easier in her mind about it if she looked out to sea in the direction of where he had been drowned. She wanted to do this. Then he spoke with his brother Galar, telling him to climb up above the door when she was going out and let a millstone fall on to her head; he said he was tired of her wailing. Galar did so. When Gilling's son, Suttung, heard of this, he went to the dwarfs and seized them and took them out to sea and put them on to a skerry covered by the tide. They begged Suttung to spare their lives offering him the precious mead as compensation for his father, and that brought about their reconciliation. Suttung took the mead home and hid it in a place called Hnitbjörg and he appointed his daughter Gunnlöd as its guardian.

This is why we call poetry Kvasir's blood, or dwarfs' drink or intoxication, or some sort of liquid of Odrörir or Bodn or Son, or dwarf's ship, because it was that mead which ransomed them from death on the skerry, or Suttung's mead or Hnitbjörg's sea.

Then Aegir spoke: 'It seems to me that it obscures to call poetry by these names.'

Yes, exactly. In introducing his discussion of the topic, Hollander notes that kennings are hardly a device unique to the old Norse skalds.

> [In their poetry] the replacement of nouns by a circumlocution is raised to a principle; or, if you please, that there is a mania for kennings, so that in extreme cases virtually nothing is mentioned by its own name or designated by an everyday word. Moreover, the rules of the art favour having one kenning built upon the other, to reach two, three, four or more storeys.

To furnish an example by no means unusual: let us say that Haki is the name of a sea-king of old. Then *haka dyr* (the animal of Haki) can stand for 'ship'; and *Haka dyrs blik* (the glamour of Haki's animal) for 'shield'—shields were fastened on the railings of the viking ship; and *Haka dyrs bliks dynr* (the tumult of the glamour of Haki's animal) for 'battle; and *Haka dyrs bliks dyns saedigr* (the gull of the tumult of the glamour of Haki's animal) for 'raven' or 'eagle'; and finally *Haka dyrs bliks dyns saediga hungrdeyfir* (the appeaser of hunger of the gulls of the tumult of the glamour of Haki's animal) for 'warrior', 'king'!

'Naturally', concludes Hollander, 'such Chinese boxes—and the one just given is not really difficult—offer endless chances for variant interpretations.'

KENNINGS ON THE EGGJUM RUNE STONE

To see just how involuted the business of kennings can get in the runic tradition itself, we can hardly do better than to study the text of a runestone found at Eggjum, Norway in 1917. Nothing about this stone is exactly certain; not its date, which some scholars place in the seventh century and others as late as 800; nor its purpose (some think it was intended as a grave marker, but the only things found under it were a knife and a flint fire-striker); nor even the literal meaning of all the words in the inscription, and certainly not the figurative meaning of those words.

Ralph Page cites an anonymously waggish Danish authority to the effect that The First Law of Runic Studies is that, for any given runic text, there shall be as many interpretations as there are runologists who have studied it. Peterson's Amendment to the First Law says that there shall be *at least* as many interpretations as runologists. If any ancient specimen were the perfect instrument for proving the truth of this facetious dictum, it would be the Eggjum Stone:

> This stone has been inlaid with the sea of the body and the wood of the sledge-runner has been shaped with it, bored with the gimlet. Which of the [rune-] horde has come here to the land of men? Against the trusty fish that swims the stream of the body, the bird screaming if he tears a corpse, is born a revenger. The stone is not reached by the sun, nor is it cut with knife. Let no man make this stone naked, nor let bold or senseless men throw it down.

Magnus Olsen gave what has become the traditional interpretation of the Eggjum runes and we shall follow that reading here, even though substantially different translations have been offered by others and are perhaps equally as plausible as Olsen's:

'Inlaid with the sea of the body'—'The sea of the body' is blood; the runemaster rubbed blood into the runes to hallow them. The use of blood in this way signifies that the runes have a magical purpose.

'The wood of the sledge-runner has been shaped with it, bored with the gimlet': The stone was dragged to its present position by a sledge, the runners of which were drilled with rope-holes, then worn down in the process of transporting the heavy stone.

'Which of the Rune-horde has come here to the land of men?': The Havamal describes how Odin sent the runes flying throughout the world so that the elves, the gods, the giants, and men all got some. This reference acknowledges the divine origin of the runes, from which they received the magical power which the runecarver is trying to invoke.

'The trusty fish that swims the stream of the body': A sword. According to Olsen, here begins a complex pun in which a name is concealed. Swords were also commonly known by the kenning of *ormr vigs* 'the serpent of battle.' 'The bird, screaming if he tears a corpse,' is the eagle. Eagles were known for their carrion-eating habits, and 'to feed the eagles' was a common kenning for killing. The serpent of battle (*orm*) plus the eagle (*ari*) combine to form the name Ormari; thus Olsen thinks the whole line is intended to be read 'Against Ormari is born an avenger.' That is (recalling that sorcerers stated their desires as if they had already been accomplished), 'let there be someone to take vengeance on Ormari.'

'The stone is not reached by the sun, nor is it cut with knife. Let no man make this stone named, nor let bold or senseless men throw it down': The stone was presumably originally hidden from sight, buried or covered in some way, and its inscriber would as soon it stayed that way. Some measure of his success in this intention may be taken from the fact that the stone was not discovered until 1917.

The reference to a knife is presumably connected to the one found buried beneath it. Both the knife and the firemaking tools had undoubtedly been hallowed in a magic rite before being placed under the stone. Their placement there also surely carried a dark symbolic meaning for the sorcerer who put up the stone. The knife is an obvious weapon; maybe the fire striker symbolized the magic maker's hopes that the avenger would burn Ormari and his family to death in their house—a common if brutal outcome in blood feuds (see, for example, the Saga of Burnt Njal; the title is self-explanatory).

SECRET RUNES

If great secrecy be equated with great magic, then the Kingigtorssuaq stone indeed be potent out of all proportion to its size. Less than three inches long, this dark greenish slate stone was found by an Eskimo on a small, rocky islet off the coast of Greenland near Upernavik in 1824. It was among three stone cairns which had apparently been built there as a landmark. The stone was shortly sent to Copenhagen, where it has been perplexing scholars ever since.

The first portion of the Kingigtorssuaq stone message is quite straightforward. Rasmus Rask made the first interpretation in 1824, and no one has seriously disputed his translation in the years since:

> Erling Sigvatsson and Bjarne Thordarson and Endrithi Oddson Saturday before 'Gangdag' raised these cairns and [ryddu?] X X X X X X[12]

The meaning of the last word, given in brackets, is controversial, and the X's at the end represent six mysterious figures which some authorities wish to read as numbers, while others see them as secret runes which conceal a word. Thalbitzer, whose interpretation of the mystery letters we shall follow here, says that 'Gangdag' can be identified from old

Figure 20: The Kigigterssuaq stener, about 3 inches long and dating from the fourteenth century, was found on the west coast of Greenland and now resides in the National Museum, Copenhagen (*from Greenlands Historiske Mindesmarker, vol. 3, Kobenhavn, 1845. pl.9*).

church calendars as 25 April, and describes runologist Finn Magnusen's opinion of that date's significance.

> [It was] a time of year when the sea between the skerries in northern Greenland is always frozen over. Thus any possibility for the three men wintering there to escape home in their vessel must have been excluded. They were obviously badly in need of help and eagerly awaiting the breaking up of the ice, which never takes place until the end of June or the beginning of July. The miserable men then must have erected the cairns, partly as signals to draw the attention of their countrymen in the south to their whereabouts and partly as an account of their expedition to be left behind if they were to perish.[13]

But, Thalbitzer says, neither Rask nor Magnusen had a plausible explanation for the last six characters of the inscription. Magnus Olsen, who provided the brilliant interpretation of the Eggjum stone cited earlier, reads the uncertain last word of the inscription before the secret runes as *ryndu*, 'wrote runes'. Another student of the Kingigtorssuaq stone, Friz Läffler, finds similarities between the six mystery characters and certain other secret runic characters from Europe which had been at least tentatively translated. Using the same system, he reads the cryptic figures of the Kingigtorssuaq as 'ice', but renders Magnusen's *rydu* as *ruddu*, taking it to mean 'cleared away'; so that the end of the inscription would read 'cleared away ice'. Thalbitzer prefers to read Magnusen's 'runed' with Läffler's 'ice'.

> There would be a clear purpose in the suggestion that the men 'runed the ice', i.e. conjured it away with runes to make the water open so that they might escape in their icebound boat from the long involuntary winter stay and go south to the home settlements.
>   The Norsemen had the same custom as the Eskimos, namely, not to mention by its true name the object to which one applies the magic, or the animal one wants to catch at sea—a king of name taboo.

I will only add that perhaps both Magnusen and Läffler are right about the meaning of the disputed last word before the secret characters. If the rune magician was able to make a pun which loaded that single word with two such appropriate meanings as 'runed' and 'cleared away' he would surely have done so, thinking thereby to condense and strengthen his magic.

NUMERIC CODING IN RUNES

The meaning of the last six characters on the Kingigtorssuaq stone is still being debated. However, several other secret rune-codes have been broken. The first of these is the bind-rune convention. Simple ones like those shown in the section on bind-runes are very common in inscriptions, and are more frequently created as abbreviations or perhaps for numero-logical purposes than as outright attempts to mystify.

In some instances, though, bind-runes can attain a level of complexity which makes them very difficult to puzzle out. Line *a* in the above figure shows the message *Ek ErilaZ* ('I, the rune-master') in normal runes. Line *b* shows this mes-sage in compound bind-runes. Lines *c* through *f* show the same message in four other types of secret runes, all based on the Aett and position numbers of the characters in the runic alphabet.

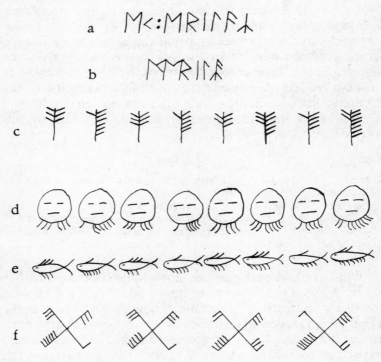

Figure 21: Secret names.

Line *c* is composed of 'twig runes' in which the number of branches to the left of the 'trunk' stave indicates the *Aett* or family, and the number of twigs to the right gives the position within the family. As with all such numbering systems, the order of the *Aettir* can be straightforward or reversed. One usually has to try reading the characters both ways in order to discover which way yields interpretable results.

Line *d* shows 'beard runes'; 'whiskers' to the left give the *Aett* number and to the right yield the position numbers. Similarly with the 'fish runes' in line *e*, the number of top fins on each fish gives the *Aett* of the rune for which it stands and the count of bottom fins reveals its position within the *Aett*.

The figures in line *f* are 'tent runes'. Each figure codes two runes. The number of branches on each arm are to be read clockwise from the top left. In the instance shown, the *Aettir* are ordered from the beginning of the alphabet to the end in 1-2-3 order. The first figure yields *Aett* 3, position 3 for the first rune and *Aett* 1, position 6 for the second. Table 1 (page 31) shows that the runes with these values are M and < : 'ek', 'I'; the second figure contains 'er', and so on.

7. DIVINATION

Let us once again quote the ancient Roman writer Tacitus on the customs of the Germanic tribes:

> To divination and the lot they pay as much attention as anyone: the method of drawing lots is uniform. A branch is cut from a nut-bearing tree [commonly hazel, beech, or oak] and divided into slips: these are distinguished by certain marks and spread casually and at random over white cloth: afterwards, if the inquiry is a public one, the priest of the state, or if private, the father of the family makes prayers to the gods and with eyes turned to heaven, takes up one slip at a time till he has done this on three separate occasions, and after taking the three interprets them according to the marks which have already been placed on each: if the message be a prohibition, no inquiry on the same matter is made for the same day; if the message be permissive, further confirmation is required by means of divination.[14]

Most scholars believe that the runes had not yet been invented in AD98, the time when Tacitus was writing. Therefore it seems that the wood-slip method of fortune telling came historically before the runes with which it was later to become so intimately associated. These early fortune-tellers marked their bits of wood with various mystical symbols such as starred circles, arrows, tree-figures, swastikas, ladders, spirals, and triangles. Some of these figures resembled runic letters and perhaps evolved into them.

In any case, it is certain that once the runes did become available, they were used as an oracle in just this way. There are many references to reading the future through the runes in the Old Norse literature and elsewhere.

Rune divination or sortilege was called *Hlautr.* This word has roots in common with modern English 'lot', in the sense of 'drawing lots'. The generic term for the wood pieces is *hlautvid,* of which there were two types. *Hlaut-tein* is usually translated 'sortilege-twig', and refers to a slip of green wood which has been cut and marked with runes for one-time use in a query. *Blot-span,* on the other hand, were chips which had been put through a consecration ritual, and which one would keep to use over and over as the need for divination might arise. *Blot* is the word for sacrifice. The two parts of the fortune-telling process were the shaking (*hrista*) and the choosing (*kiosa*) of the *hlaut-vid.*

The Landnama Bok gives several instances in which *Hlautr* was practised. 'Of the two rivals, Eanwind and Eric, Eanwind cast the hallowed chips to know when Eric was going to set out to capture the contested valley.' With his advance knowledge of his enemy's movements, Eanwind was able to carry the day and win the land for himself. Another passage tells how the Swedes cast the *Blot-Span* to find out how to end a famine—an occurrence which brings to mind the incident from Eirik the Red's Saga (recounted in an earlier chapter) in which questions were put to a *volva* in Greenland.

Sometimes the object of the query was more trivial. A king of the Swedes is reported to have made sacrifice and used the chips to find his lost pet.

In the following lines at the beginning of the *Hymiskvitha* the Gods themselves consult the runes in order to find out where to go for more party supplies when they had finished off what they had on hand:

> Of old the gods
>   made feast together
> And drink they sought
>   ere sated they were;
> Twigs they shook
>   and blood they tried:
> Thus mead in Aegir's
>   hall they found.

Two notes of explanation are in order: 'blood' presumably refers to the sacrifices they made in order to consecrate the runes. Aegir was a sea-giant in the Germanic legends who had some of the attributes of the Greek god Poseidon.

Figure 22: Wooden runes with burnt-on characters, kept in a small bag.

READING THE RUNES

The modern user may adopt the method outlined by Tacitus, perhaps securing a cloth of plain white cotton to spread the runes out on. Others keep their runes in a small bag of unbleached muslin or wool and consult them by drawing three out one at a time for study.

A CONSECRATION CEREMONY

We recall from the chapter on the old Germanic world-view that the Teutonic peoples believed not only in the gods and goddesses of their pantheon, Odin, Thor, Frey, Freyja, Tyr, and so on, but also in a pervasive force in nature similar to the *mana* of the Polynesians. They called this force *megin* and held it to be the active principle which causes magical acts to have their effect. It is through the *Megin* of the Norns by which the divinatory rite is tied to the events in the future which are to be predicted.

In order to activate *megin*, ancient tradition required that a rune set be 'charged with power' or consecrated by some sort of sacrifice before being used to foretell the future. The blood mentioned in the *Hymiskvitha* lines above is a reference to an animal sacrifice; the creature's blood was sprinkled on the runes to hallow them. You won't need to kill anything in order to 'charge' your runes, however. It will suffice if you take your rune set with you to a nearby body of water, throw three coins into the water and hold up the runes, saying three times, 'I give these coins to the three Norns. Let the runes speak true'. You may substitute some phrase such as 'the God-Force' if you are uncomfortable with the idea of making sacrifice to the Norns. Repeat the offering and prayer three times so a total of nine coins and nine prayers have been offered. The number nine is a powerful one in rune lore. Note that Odin hung on the tree of Yggdrasil for nine nights to earn knowledge of the runes, and Mimir gave him nine power-songs.

SETTING THE SCENE

The rune reader usually begins with a quiet moment of meditation to create a mental framework for posing a question. It is a good idea to invoke spiritual protection at such a time: simply ask whatever helpful spirits you might happen to believe in (or perhaps the creative aspect of the universe itself) to surround you with a field which will keep you from harm, and then visualize such a field taking form around you.

The question may either be written down on a piece of paper or simply held in mind as the runes are drawn. Avoid agonizing unduly over the precise wording of your query: in fact, the question need not even be in verbal form: some people find it sufficient to hold in mind a sort of wordless 'sense of the problem'.

THE RUNES SPEAK

The *first* rune to be drawn defines the **present situation** and the *third* a **potential outcome**, while the *second* describes the **process or action** by which the situation of the first rune might evolve into the outcome pictured in the third.

Sometimes a rune reading is best interpreted as providing advice on how to get from a present condition to a desired outcome; at other times it seems to give a warning about the consequence of some action, and there are times when it appears to report an inexorable course of events. If the first rune seems not to fit the present situation, then perhaps it is trying to draw your attention to some aspect of the situation which you are ignoring (or of which you are unaware).

Each person must learn by experience and the repeated exercise of intuition just how rune readings are to be interpreted. As you grow more familiar with the rich texture of runic symbolism, as you immerse yourself in the spirit of the runes, you will become more adept at understanding the messages you are receiving.

Some examples might be useful here. For the first, I focused my mind on the need for such an example and drew three oaken runes one by one from the bag in which I store them.

The first rune was RAIÐU, the Chariot. This suggests that the issue at hand has to do with communication. The reader should turn to the meaning listed for that rune (page 107) and muse a bit on other aspects of the rune's meaning as they relate to my need for an example. Do you see anything having to do with human productivity or creativity, or community among people?

The second rune I drew was BERKANA (page 123) and the third was INGWAZ (page 127). You may want to go ahead and look up these runes first and put together your own interpretation before I offer mine.

Let us now proceed: does it seem to you, as it does to me, that the meaning of these three runes must be somewhat as follows? RAIÐU says that the present situation has to do with communication, with a need to lead others toward a skill that is essentially creative in nature. BERKANA indicates that this may proceed through a regeneration, as new shoots might grow from an ancient root, just as this book seeks to start new growth from the ancient root of the runic tradition. INGWAZ may be read to mean that the end state of the sequence is serenity and contact with the higher self.

In a second instance, a student whose existence seemed to have stagnated asks, 'Is there a dominant theme in my life at this time?' and receives the following reading:

MANNAZ directs the inquirer's attention to thoughts of human frailties, TIWAZ to the idea of victory through brave action, and IWAZ points to resilient strength.

I believe that the MANNAZ rune suggests that the inquirer is trapped in his present stagnation due to aspects of his own character which need further development. TIWAZ counsels him to honestly and bravely confront those aspects of his nature which prevent his success and thereby release himself from his personal morass. IWAZ, the rune of strength through adversity, holds out the promise, not of an end to problems, but of increased strength to overcome them as a reward for his courageous acts of self-discovery and change.

Let us go on to examine a reading done for a woman who was thinking of pursuing a Ph.D. in counselling psychology. Her own American Indian background and experiences in therapy had given her certain new insights about the problems of Native Americans. She believed she could develop these ideas into a treatment programme and write up the result for her thesis. However, she was at a stage of life in which her other responsibilities would make doctoral studies exceptionally difficult.

The runes GEBU, JARA, and DAGAZ arose in a reading for her. I take this reading to indicate that the doctoral path is open to her, but it will entail initial sacrifices. These hardships lead directly to benefits to the society and finally to personal fulfilment.

For a last example, a businessman had to make a timing decision on the introduction of a new product. He was uncertain whether it would be better to introduce the item immediately to get a lead on possible competition or to plan for an autumn release, when sales are traditionally better. The rune reading gave SOWELU, TIWAZ, and ODALA.

SOWELU (life force, vitality, rationality) seems to indicate that the product is well conceived and potentially viable in the marketplace. TIWAZ calls for bold and deliberate action, promising victory against a foe. ODALA speaks of inheritance and essences of things, of acquiring that which is one's due. The runes seem to clearly call for immediate release so that a good product might claim its rightful place in a competitive market.

KEEP A LOG

I strongly suggest that anyone who wishes to become seriously involved with the runes should keep a written log of his or her transactions with the rune oracle, recording at least the theme of each query and the answer received.

When you begin working with the runes, you will sometimes be puzzled by the responses you get. You must keep in mind, however, that a confusing signal from the runes is not necessarily wrong. Sometimes the runes are reacting to aspects of the situation which are not yet apparent to you. You will be able to improve your interpretive skills and deepen your understanding of messages only if you can go back after the fact and see how the readings tie to later events.

'SLEEPING ON' A READING

Do not be too hasty to give up on a reading if it does not seem to make immediate sense. Try 'sleeping on' a difficult rune cast. That is, just before you go to sleep you should clear your mind of other thoughts and peacefully bring to mind the meaning of the first rune. If possible, create a visualization of that meaning.

When you get the meaning of the rune clearly in mind, mentally set it aside and replace it with a representation of the second rune. Work on this rune in the same way, and then the third rune. Keep bringing the three runes to mind in sequence until you drift off to sleep. They will come to mind with greater and greater ease as you program your unconscious to work on them.

In the morning you should first try to remember any dreams you had during the night. Then turn to your log, which you left, perhaps on your dresser, open to the page of the problem reading. Try again to interpret the runes, and the odds are that you will experience a rush of new insights.

The drawings in this book can be used as visualization aids for many of the runes.

VARIATIONS

In addition to the traditional three-rune method of divination, some people use the runes as if they were Tarot cards, placing them carved-side downward in various layouts and turning them up one by one to be read. Incidentally, there are some fascinating similarities and differences between the runic and the Tarot symbologies which will be of interest to any student of such matters.

Also by analogy with the Tarot, some rune readers attend to whether the rune is right-side-up or not in the spread. If the rune is reversed, so is its meaning. Some runes, such as NAUÐIZ and INGWAZ, cannot be reversed and therefore have no inverted meaning. Also, the rune ALGIZ was written upside down in some versions of the Futhark, so if you are going to give special meanings to inversions of the runes it would probably be a good idea to include ALGIZ among the runes which cannot be reversed. Anyone who wants to use the runes in this way can consult one of the many excellent books available on the Tarot.

It is worthwhile to note that, even without attending to reversals, the traditional three-rune reading is capable of generating 12,144 different messages from a 24-character set, or 13,800 messages if the blank rune is added. These numbers should be compared to the 4096 mutually distinct messages possible with the Chinese divining method, the *I Ching*.

Learning to read the runes well is neither an easy nor an instant process; your skill will grow in accordance with the amount of study, thought, and practice you put in. I believe that there is sufficient challenge for most of us in learning to make valid interpretations of these twelve or thirteen thousand possible messages. Unless you have a very well thought-out reason for wanting to blend such disparate traditions I see no particular advantage to getting involved in Tarot spreads, consideration of reversed characters and similar departures from the customary rune methods, for I expect that these needless complications will often prove to be more distracting than useful.

PART TWO:
THE MEANINGS OF THE RUNES

ᚠ

FEHU
Cattle, Money

This rune refers to wealth or worldly goods in the purely physical sense: material possessions, prosperity, money, profits, moveable property in general (as opposed to real estate). The English word 'fee' is an etymological relative of FEHU.

Cattle were symbols of material wealth among the Germanic tribes, just as they were among the Romans, whose word for money (*pecunia*) is derived from the Latin word for cow (*pecus*). To this day, wealth among many African peoples is reckoned in cattle.

ᚢ

URUS
The Aurochs

URUS represents great strength, in either the physical or spiritual sense. Applied to the mundane world, it can refer to physical strength or to the strength of will necessary to overcome obstacles and opposition in reaching a goal. In a more metaphysical sense, it describes a spiritual 'force' or principle which pervades the world and which gives sorcerers, the lesser spirits, and the gods themelves their mysterious powers. Scandinavians called this principle *megin* and the Polynesians call it *mana*.

The Aurochs was a gigantic variety of wild ox, standing as high as seven feet at the shoulder. It became extinct when the last of the species died in Poland in 1627.

THURISAZ
Giant/Demon

The giants were the traditional enemies of the gods in the Germanic religion. Subterranean beings, they were believed to control the fierce and destructive elements: the frosts of winter, earthquakes, volcanoes, etc.

This rune may refer literally to these elemental forces of nature, but can also symbolize destructive aspects of the personality such as irrational or excessive anger and fears: the blind 'subterranean' forces of the human unconscious. The Skirnismal poem of the Poetic Edda described how Freyr's servant Skirnir wrote three THURISAZ runes to create a charm which brought 'longing and madness and lust'. The female menstrual cycle ('the torment of women' in a Norwegian rune-poem) was also thought to be in the domain of the THURISAZUR.

ᚠ

ANSUZ
A God; Odin

Wisdom; power through knowledge; mastery of the self and of occult matters.

> Mind-runes learn,
>   if thou shalt become
> Wiser than all other men.
> —*Sigrdrifumal*

This is the shaman's sign. It has to do with the individual's quest for wisdom, and the sacrifices which lie in the path of one who seeks self-knowledge. Literally, ANSUZ is the old singular form of Aesir. Odin is the king of the Aesir, master-magician and clairvoyant, but even he had to pay dearly for his powers. He not only subjected himself to the vision quest ordeal described in preceding pages, but also gave one of his eyes to gain wisdom.

> A better burden
>   may no man bear
>   for wanderings wide than wisdom;
> It is better than wealth
>   on unknown ways
>   and in grief a refuge it gives.
> —*Havamal*

The student of the occult may want to compare the meaning of this rune with the conventional interpretation given the Hanged Man of the Tarot cards.

R   RAIÐU   5
Chariot

The chariot of the sun, the ceremonial wagon of the fertility rite. This rune indicates speedy travel, the sending of messages, human productivity, and by extension to modern circumstances, electronic communications.

To the ancients, the chariot was associated with the yearly fertility ceremony, that special time of year when the gods were believed to be travelling about among the mortals who worshipped them. This was always a time of peace, reverence, rejoicing as the wagon with its retinue passed from one community to the next, bearing news and gossip, hopes for prosperity, and a sense of community among men which was rather rare in the normally fragmented early Germanic society with its multitudinous bickering and blood-feuding factions.

Ceremonial wagons have been found in burial mounds and ship burials; it is wrong, however, to conclude that these wagons were therefore primarily associated with funeral rites. Instead, it is likely that the tradition was for a chieftain-priest to be buried with his ship, weapons, and ritual wagon accompanying him as tokens of the roles he played in life as a sea-adventurer, warrior, and pagan priest.

The other runes are named for gods, animals, natural forces, etc. This is the only one which describes a manufactured device. Whereas the sun-rune indicates vitality and potential, RAIÐU, the carrier of the sun symbol, represents these potentials brought into concrete physical existence. It is therefore the rune of human activity and movement, the symbol of creating and transmitting information, of the manufacturing and production of goods.

> Arvak and Alsvith*
>   up shall drag
>   The weary weight of the sun;
> But an iron cool**
>   have the kindly gods
>   Of yore set under their yokes.
>
> In front of the sun
>   does Svalin stand,
>   The shield of the shining god;†
> Mountains and sea
>   would be set in flames
>   If it fell from before the sun.

*Arvak ('Early-waker') and Alsvith ('All-swift') are the names of the horses who draw the chariot.
**'An iron cool' is in other references described as a bellows which blows cool air on the animals.
†The shining god is Freyr, who was often represented as riding the sun-chariot in the fertility rite.

Illustration: The Oseberg Wagon, from the Viking Ships Museum, Oslo, Norway.

KAUNA
Canker, sore

A physical or mental affliction; melancholy, or distress. Something which will get worse if left unattended; an unfinished healing process.

Some writers give *candle* or *torch* as an alternative meaning for this rune, perhaps through an expansion of 'inflammation' into a *double entendre* containing both its literal and figurative senses.

Illustration: A monster depicted on one of the sledges found in the Oseberg Ship. Now in the Viking Ships Museum, Oslo, Norway.

X   GEBU   7
Gift/Sacrifice

GEBU may mean either an ordinary gift such as you might give or receive from another, or a sacrifice which you must make in order to accomplish something.

Of ordinary gifts between people the *Havamal* says:

> No great thing needs
>   a man to give;
>   Oft little will purchase praise.
> With half a loaf
>   and a half-filled cup
>   A friend full fast I made.

And of sacrifices made to the gods it advises:

> 'Tis better not to pray
>   than too much offer;
>   A gift always calls for gift,
> Better give none
>   than too big a sacrifice.

GEBU is one of the runes which were commonly invoked in prosperity charms.

Illustration: A Slavanic silver earring and bracteate from the State Historical Museum in Stockholm, Sweden. The silver necklet and gold amulet are from Vullum in northern Norway.

ᚹ

WUNJU
Joy

WUNJU can mean joy or happiness in the conventional sense, but more importantly it has the additional meaning of the ecstatic state which one may enter through means such as meditation and fasting.

The person who has learned to shut out the outside world and find this interior ecstacy has found a doorway to wisdom through mastery of the self.

Sigrdrifa, the Valkyrie who taught the runes to the hero Sigurd, said:

> First I will bring
>   beer to the warrior—
>   Might brewed it, mingled it with fame—
> Full of spells
>   and potent songs,
>
>   Rich in charms and runes of joy.

ᚺ

HAGALAZ
Hail

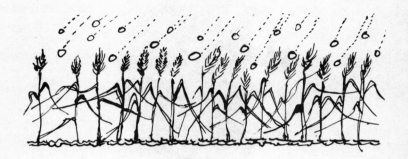

Disruptive forces of nature; a setback due to events beyond your control. Even though a person cannot directly control the course of the event indicated by HAGALAZ, it is important to analyse what is happening because one who understands the situation can take actions which will mitigate the effects of the event.

The HAGALAZ rune may be a warning to make advance preparations for adversity.

To an agricultural people, hail is a symbol of the recurring and uncontrollable disasters which can ruin a crop and cause a lean year from time to time, but such misfortune will not be fatal to those who have prepared themselves with emergency stores.

NAUÐIZ
Need

Literal need or want; constraint; affliction; a stumbling-block; imposition of a restraint. Drawing this rune sometimes means a need for temperance in one's behaviour.

NAUÐIZ was used in a legendary protection rite to restrain another's evil intentions.

> Ale-runes learn,
>   that with lies the wife
>   Of another betray not thy trust;
> On the horn thou shalt write,
>   and the backs of thy hands,
>   And NAUÐIZ shalt thou mark on thy nails.
>
> Thou shalt bless the draught
>   and danger escape
>   And cast a leek in the cup;
> For so I know
>   thou never shalt see
>   Thy mead with evil mixed.

Obscure as this verse sounds to us, it was clear enough to a Norseman. As Bellows interprets it, a guest who visited the hall of another was greeted with a horn of ale from his host's wife, 'and it was to prevent this draught from bewitching him that the runes were recommended'. The verse quote for Rune 21, LAUKZ, provides additional advice for this social situation.

I
ISAZ
Ice

Standstill; a 'freezing up' of your affairs, usually of a temporary nature. A barren or wintery period. Also chilling, cooling off, loss of ardour, etc.

A Norseman drawing this rune might have imagined his longship locked into a frozen fjord and realized that in good time the warm days of spring would come to release him. The small Kingigtorssuaq Runestone found in Greenland is thought by some to have been carved by a frozen-in party of Icelandic adventurers in a magical effort to 'rune away' the ice.

JARA
(Bountiful) Year

A bountiful harvest, a prosperous time. The sense is more that of commonly shared good fortune, as when the national or world economy is thriving, than of a more limited, personal variety of good luck. The meaning of this rune is directly opposed to that of the previous one, ISAZ.

It was in order to obtain the blessing of JARA, a prosperous year (or season), that the ancients held their fertility rites. They often carved isolated (or trebled) JARA runes as charms to invoke abundance in their crops and animals.

> Hope not too surely
> for early harvest,
> Nor trust too soon in thy son;
> The field needs good weather,
> the son needs wisdom,
> And oft is either denied.
> —Havamal

Illustration: Carving on a chair from Viking period in a church in Bö, Norway.

ᛇ IWAZ 13
Yew, Bow

Resilient strength; ability to deflect difficulty, or a problem warded off.

The yew is a tree in the pine family, quite similar to the North American hemlock in appearance. Its brilliant dark green needles stand out the most strikingly of all the trees in the deathly white of the northern winter: thus the tree came to symbolize resistance to adversity. Also, yew wood was the most favoured material for making a warrior's bow, a fact which reinforced the associated values of toughness and resilience.

Two additional meanings for this rune are *sorrow* and *poison*. The former meaning probably derives from the custom of planting yew trees in graveyards, while the latter derives from a poisonous alkaloid contained in yew foliage.

ᛈ PERÐRA/PERU 14
Pear(?)

Something unknown, occult, or not yet revealed or which remains unresolved; a mystery in the same sense that an unborn child is a mystery. A secret, a birth, a material gain or loss to be realized in due time.

> Birth-runes learn,
> if help thou wilt lend,
> The babe from the mother to bring;
> On thy palms shalt write them,
> and round thy joints
> And ask the *disir* to aid.
> —*Sigrdrifumal*

This rune is a difficult one. The name PERÐRA is the conventional reconstruction of the early Germanic name of this rune. Although PERÐRA is one of the runes which dropped out of the Scandinavian Futhark by about AD 800, it persisted in the English runes, where it was called PEORÐ. I commented on page 9 that this word is known only as a rune-name and has no other identified meaning in Anglo-Saxon or Old English. However, Eric Oxenstierna, a Swedish student of the proto-Scandinavian runic tradition, identifies its meaning as 'fruit tree'.[15] The most plausible linguistic association between the fruit tree concept and a word like PERÐRA in the old Germanic tongue seems to me to be the pear (*PERU*). I therefore suggest the latter as the source of the rune-name. The associated meanings having to do with pregnancy derive the the womb-like shape of the pear and from the notion of 'bearing fruit'. Also note the pearlike shape of the ancient fertility figures such as the 'Venus of Willendorf'.

Yggdrasil, the 'universe tree', is a sort of magnet which draws all the symbolism toward itself. The following two stanzas from the Svipdagsmal poem, although they clearly refer to Yggdrasil in their recorded form, may have their root in an earlier pear tree context, and thus give some tentative confirmation to the interpretations I suggest. The Svipdagsmal is a relatively late poem, in which self-conscious literary concerns sometimes overshadow the original mythic material.

> Now answer me, Fjolsvith,
>   the question I ask,
> For now the truth would I know:
> What grows from the seed
>   of the tree so great
> That fire nor iron shall fell?

> Women, sick
>   with child, shall seek
> Its fruit to the flames to bear;
> Then out shall come
>   what within was hid,
> Revealing its portents for men.

The eccentric German rune enthusiast Carl Schneider thinks this rune means 'dice cup'.[16] Page accuses Schneider of 'misplaced erudition.'[17] Even so, it is interesting that the dice cup idea yields an extending meaning very similar to what I have suggested above; both the dice box and the womb preserve their secrets for a time.

ᛉ ALGIZ **15**
European Elk

Luck in the hunt; a successful outcome to a quest. This rune has the specific meaning of success through striving, or reward through effort, rather than the sort of good luck which one might merely fall into.

The European elk is the same animal (Alcis alcis) which an American or Canadian would call a moose. ALGIZ is surely one of the oldest of the culture symbols among the runes, and perhaps the only one to be a stylized representation of its namesake, if the three ascending 'tines' are thought of as the antlers of the animal. Stone Age hunting and gathering cultures in Scandinavia sculpted many game animals out of stone and carved their outlines on rocky cliffs to bring luck in the hunt. Elk, the largest of these game animals, were the most common subjects of the early magician-artists.

Popular writers such as Lord[18] follow a later Anglo-Saxon tradition to give meanings of *protection, sacrifice,* or *a new interest* to this rune, but these meanings come from a different Germanic root word and a time long after the original significance of ALGIZ had been forgotten.

Illustration: Greenstone ape with the hand of an elk from Alunda, Uppland, c. *2000 BC.* (Courtesy of the Historical Museum, Stockholm).

ᛉ

SOWELU
Sun

Life force, vitality, the light of truth, human consciousness, rationality. Power to calm the sea or to make a sea voyage safe.

The chariot of the gods was often depicted among the Germanic peoples as carrying a sun-disc or mandala, a universal symbol for the sun, the higher self, wholeness.

> Wave-runes learn,
>   if well thou wouldst shelter
> The sail-steeds out on the sea;
> On the stem shalt thou write,
>   and the steering-blade,
> And brand them into the oars;
> Though high be the breakers,
>   and black the waves,
> Thou shalt safe the harbour
> seek.

Illustration: A bronze and gold sun chariot and horse, 60cm long, found at Trundholm, Seeland, Denmark.

TIWAZ
God of Bravery

Victory in legal, political, or physical combat; disputation.
TIWAZ was the bravest, and one of the wisest, of the gods.
It was said of him that he was not known as a peace-bringer.
He oversaw battle and meetings of the *Thing*, the combined
courtroom and legislative body of the Germanic tribes. His
rune is commonly taken to signify victory in combat or in
the courtroom—two arenas which the Germanic peoples saw
as quite similar, all in all.

> Speech-runes learn,
>   that none may seek
> To answer harm with hate;
> Well he winds
>   and weaves them all
> And sets them side by side,
> At the judgement-place,
>   when justice there
> The folk shall fairly win.

The Viking poem *Sigrdrifumal* advises:

> Victory-runes learn
>   if thou seekest to win
> And the runes
> On thy sword-hilt scratch:
>   some in the channel
> And some on the flat,
> And twice call on TIWAZ.

TiwaZ got his reputation for bravery during an incident when the gods were seeking to chain the wolf Fenris. The only chain which would hold the wolf was a magic one which the dwarfs made from the noise of a cat, a woman's beard, the breath of a fish, and a bird's spittle. Fenris would only permit himself to be bound with it while he held a god's hand in his mouth as a pledge. TiwaZ volunteered his hand and lost it rather than let the wolf go free again.

The name TiwaZ is related to the Greek Zeus and the Latin Deus. Scholars believe that TiwaZ was the Germanic version of the Indo-European sky god, and was originally the most important of the gods. However, as the cult of Odin gained strength among the nordic peoples, Odin's worshippers appropriated many of TiwaZ's attributes for their favoured god.

Illustration: A Viking sword in the Bergen Museum, Norway.

BERKANA
Birch tree

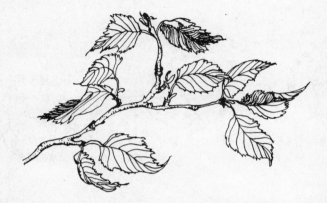

Healing; recovery; physical or spiritual regeneration; renewal; a new growth from old roots.

These meanings arise partly from the observation that if a birch tree is cut down, new shoots will grow from the stump. The healing aspect of the birch symbol is reinforced by the fact that birch twigs contain a chemical closely related to aspirin and are a common ingredient in the folk medicines of many Northern peoples, including the American Indians.

Berkana is the 'branch rune' referred to in the following lines of an Old Norse poem:

> Branch-runes know
>   if to leechwork
>   Thou wouldst turn
>   and healing balms would make.
> On the bark thou shalt spell,
>   and on trees that grow
>   With limbs to
>   the eastward turned.

Leechwork means the art of healing. The runes were carved into the bark of the tree in order to transfer the illness from the patient to the tree.

ᛗ EHWAZ
Horse

This rune means travel in the literal sense, but can also refer to travel on what modern occultists call the 'astral plane'. In particular, EHWAZ can refer both to precognition, the sort of mental 'travel' by which one acquires knowledge of the future, and to travel to the Spirit World, implying communication with world of the dead.

According to Tacitus, the ancient Germans kept sacred horses which they used for divination, allowing nobody outside the priesthood to touch them. The priests were reputed to understand the language of neighs and snorts by which the horses told them of what was to come.

MANNAZ
Man

The self; a human being or the human race; human frailty or untrustworthiness; distrust of oneself or others. 'Yet', says an Anglo-Saxon rune poem, 'each is bound to fail his fellow'. Although this interpretation may sound to some like a Christian addition (the original Peter Principle, perhaps? Mark 14:66-72), the Havamal has many interesting things to say about trust among men, such as:

> If another thou hast
>   whom thou hardly wilt trust,
>   Yet good from him wouldst get,
> Thou shalt speak him fair,
>   but falsely think
>   And fraud with falsehood requite.

> Away from his arms
>   in the open field
>   A man should fare not afoot;
> For he never knows
>   when the need of a spear
>   Shall arise on the distant road.

Illustration: Figures from stamps used for impressing bronze plates such as helmets found in Vendel grave sites, Uppland, Sweden. They date from the sixth to the ninth century AD.

ᛚ

LAUKZ
Leek

A healing herb, a balm; shielding from the malice of others; psychic or physical protection. The leek was thought to neutralize poisons. It also represents the male principle; sexual potency.

Both English and Icelandic sources give LAGUZ, Lake or Water as the meaning for this rune, and some writers suppose it to have the extended meaning of 'Intuition'. However, it seems likely that this was a relatively late amendment to the rune names, inspired by the Christian church because the leek was not only a healing herb, but was a phallic symbol as well among the old Teutons and their immediate descendants.

A Valkyrie teaches the hero Sigurd the use of the runes, advising him:

> Thou shalt bless the
> draught,
>   and danger escape,
>   And cast a leek in the cup;
> For so I know
>   thou never shalt see
>   Thy mead with evil mixed.

Illustration: A silver beaker, 9.7cm high, from Fejo, Denmark, dating from about AD 800, in the National Museum, Copenhagen.

◇

INGWAZ
Fertility god

Peace and bounty in the external world; physical sensuality, romantic love; serenity as applied to questions of the human spirit.

INGWAZ is another name for the god Freyr, to whom worship and sacrifices were dedicated in the interest of securing a good harvest and bringing peace.

It was a custom among the nordic peoples to give each child a gift to mark the emergence of his or her first tooth. The other gods gave to Freyr the realm of Alfheim, home of the light-elves, as his tooth-gift. Freyr, also had a magic, shining sword which could fight by itself. He mostly used this sword to fight against the frost-giants. The dwarfs gave him a golden boar which tore up the earth with its tusks and thus taught mankind how to till the earth. The boar with its golden bristles was a personification of the sun, and the magic sword seems to have symbolized the rays of the sun, thus explaining its effectiveness against the frost-giants.

Freyr was often represented in images as having an immense erect penis, a symbol of fertility and amourousness. People sacrificed a boar to him at the Yule celebrations to obtain prosperity in the coming year (JARA).

Illustration: 7cm bronze sculpture of Freyr from 'Rällinge, Södermanland, Sweden — now in the Historiske Museum, Stockholm.

DAGAZ
Day

Opportunity; the present moment; change for the better; turning point.

In contrast with JARA, DAGAZ carries with it a sense of immediacy. The inquirer who receives this rune is perhaps being advised to seize the moment, to take some immediate action regarding the topic of the inquiry.

> Speak forth, gain-wizard,
>   if there from the floor
> Thou wouldst thy wisdom make known:
> What name has the steed
>   that each morn anew
> The day for mankind doth draw?

> Skinfaxi* is he,
>   the steed who for men
> The glittering day doth draw;
> The best of horses
>   to heroes he seems,**
> And brightly his mane doth burn.

> Speak forth, gain-wizard,
>   if there from the floor
> Thou wouldst thy wisdom make known:
> What name has the steed
>   that from east anew
> Brings night for the noble gods?

Hrimfaxi name they
   the steed that anew
 Brings night for the noble gods;
Each morning foam
   from his bit there falls,
And thence come the dews in the dales.
          —*Vafthrudnismal*

*Skinfaxi means 'shining mane'; Hrimfaxi means 'frosted mane'.
** 'The best of horses to heroes he seems': Each day is a new opportunity for great deeds and victories.

Illustration: Ship from the Gotlandic picture-stone, Liddare, Hynam Parish, Sweden, c. AD 800.

OÐALA
Ancestral land

Inheritance, ancestral homeland; retreat or the place to which one retreats. OÐALA can also stand for the individual's inner nature or essence, or for 'inheritance' in the genetic sense of a hereditary trait.

> Better a house,
> though a hut it be,
> A man is master at home;
> A pair of goats
> and a patched-up roof
> Are better far than begging.
> —*Havamal*

Odal rights amounted to an absolute title to land in the old Germanic common law; *odala* land could not be seized from the owner, who was termed an *odalbondi*. The law had many provisions which were intended to preserve ownership for the *odalbondi* and his descendants. For example, if *odal* land was sold outside the family, the nearest of kin retained the right to redeem the land within a specified time and under certain conditions.

According to the law in one region, for example, the rule was that the kinsmen of the *bondi* who had sold the land could repossess the land after paying an amount one-fifth less than the value of the land as appraised by disinterested arbitrators. The law specified that the redemption payment was to be made half in gold and silver and half in male thralls (slaves) 'not older than forty and not younger than fifteen winters'. In order to keep this option open, though, the kinsman had to publicly announce his *odal* rights at the meeting of the district *Thing* within twenty years after the sale, and to repeat this declaration down through the years so that twenty years should never be allowed to pass between two announcements.

But even if the next of kin allowed twenty years to expire without making the announcement, he did not forfeit all redemption rights, but had to pay the full assessed value in order to reclaim it. Only after land had been in the family of the purchaser for sixty years without kinsmen of the old owner announcing their redemption rights did the land become *odala* of the new owner.

APPENDIX

Phonetic Spelling with Runes

The twenty-four original runes were designed as a system for writing the old common Germanic language, and they served this purpose well. However, modern English has evolved into a substantially different language and, most importantly, the sound system has undergone considerable change. Also, English spelling is notoriously different from pronunciation.

Animal head wood carving from the Oseberg ship. The headpost dates from the fourth or fifth century and is now in the Viking Ship House, Bygdöy, Oslo (from Sheteling, Haakon & Falk, 1978: pp293-5).

For these reasons, if you try it you will soon discover that any attempt to simply make a letter-by-letter substitution of Roman to runic characters in English words is useless. For example, it would make no sense to spell 'isle' as ᛁᛋᛚᛖ in Runic. Instead, you would use ᚠᛁᛚ, and of course you would use the same runic spelling for 'aisle' (but should spell out abbreviations, so 'I'll' would be ᚨᛁ : ᚹᛁᛚ, 'I will'). The phonetic system offered here has some awkwardness, but generally you can make it work. You can make minor changes as needed to satisfy a numerological formula or to invest a spell with the power of a favoured rune meaning (perhaps ᚢᛋᚺᚾ instead of ᚹᛋᚺᚾ for 'wish' if your purpose favours using URUZ instead of WUNJU).

VOWELS

Letter	Sound	Runic Form
A	far	ᚠ
	sad	ᚠᛗ
	grade	ᛗᛁ
E	meet	ᛁ
	led	ᛗ
I	hid	ᛋ
	hide	ᚾᛁ
O	odd	ᚠ
	over	ᛟ
U	up	ᚢ
	fluke	ᚢᛈ
Y	yes	ᛁ

REGULAR CONSONANTS

B ᛒ	D ᛞ	F ᚠ	H ᚺ
J ᛃ	K ᚲ	L ᚱ	M ᛗ
N ᚾ	Ng ᛜ	p ᛈ	R ᚱ
T ᛏ	Th ᚦ	W ᚹ	Z ᛉ

Observe that in two cases, sounds which require two letters ('Th' and 'Ng', above) in the modern alphabet are represented by single runic characters. Thus 'thing' would be ᚦᛁᛜ in the Runic system.

IRREGULAR CONSONANTS

Letter	Sound	Rune
C	city	ᛋ
	can	ᚲ
Ch	child	ᛏᛋᚺ
G	go	ᚷ
	ginger	ᛃ
Qu	quit	ᚲᚹ
S	sing	ᛋ
	his	ᛉ
Sh	shoe	ᛋᚺ
V	very	ᚠ̇
X	text	ᚲᛋ

There is no runic equivalent for the English V sound. We solve this problem by creating a new character, the dotted FEHU, ᚠ̇, to represent the V as a 'voiced F'. For magical purposes, its symbolic and numerological values are identical with the conventional FEHU.

NOTES

1. H.R. Ellis Davidson, *Gods and Myths*, 1964.
2. C. Tacitus, Germania, 1914.
3. H.A. Bellows (Trans.), *Poetic Edda*, 1969.
4. J. Kohl, *Kitchi-Gami*, 1985.
5. W. McDougall, *Body and Mind*, 1974.
6. J. Piaget, *Child's Conception of the World*, 1967.
7. A.I. Hallowell, *Culture and Experience*, 1955.
8. W. James, *Principles of Psychology* (Vol.1), 1890.
9. C.G. Jung, *Synchronicity*, 1973.
10. J. Frazer, *Golden Bough*, 1929.
11. B. Malinowski, *Magic, Science and Religion*.
12. Cited in W. Thalbitzer, *Two Runic Stones*, 1951.
13. Thalbitzer, *op. cit.*
14. Tacticus, *op. cit.*
15. E. Oxenstierna, *The Norsemen*, 1965.
16. K. Schneider, *Germanische Runenamen*, 1956.
17. R. I. Page, *English Runes*, 1956,
18. G. Lord, 'Your furure in the Runes', 1983.

BIBLIOGRAPHY

Andersen, Harry. 'Om urnordisk erilaẐ og jarl,' *Sprog og Kultur*, 16: 97-102, 1948.

Andersen, Harry. *Runologica: Harry Andersens Udvalgte runologiske afhandlinger* (Copenhagen: Akademisk Forlag, 1952).

Anderson, Rasmus B. *Norse Mythology* (7th Ed.) (Chicago: Scott, Foresman, 1907).

Antonsen, Elmer. *A Concise Grammar of the Older Runic Inscriptions* (Tübingen, Germany: Niemeyer Verlag, 1975).

Arntz, Helmut. *Handbuch der Runenkunde* (Halle-Saale: Niemeyer, 1935).

Baeksted, Anders. *Maalruner og troldruner: Runemagiske studier* (Copenhagen: Nordisk Forlag, 1952).

Becker, Alfred. *Franks Casket: Zu den Bildern ind Inschriften des Runenkästchens von Auzon* (Nuremburg: Hans Carl Verlag, 1973).

Bellows, Henry Adams (Trans.). *The Poetic Edda* (New York: Biblo & Tannen, 1969).

Branston, Brian. *Gods of the North* (New York: Vanguard).

Branston, Brian. *The Lost Gods of England* (New York: Oxford University Press, 1974).

Du Chaillu, Paul. *The Viking Age* (2 vols.) (New York: Scribner's Sons, 1889).

Dumezil, Georges. *Gods of the Ancient Northmen* (Einar Haugen, Ed. & Trans.) (Berkeley: University of California Press, 1973).

Düwel, Klaus. *Runenkunde* (Stuttgart: J.B. Metzlersche Verlagsbuchhandlung, 1968).

Einarsson, Stefan. *Icelandic: Grammar, Texts, Glossary* (Baltimore: Johns Hopkins University Press, 1945).

Ellis Davidson, Hilda R. *Gods and Myths of Northern Europe* (Harmondsworth: Penguin, 1964).

Ellis Davidson, Hilda R. *Pagan Scandinavia* (New York: Praeger, 1967).

Foote, Peter G. and Wilson, David M. *The Viking Achievement* (New York: Praeger, 1970).

Frazer, James G. *The Golden Bough* (2 vols.) (New York: Book League of America, 1929).

Gordon, E.V. *An Introduction to Old Norse* (2nd Ed. Rev. A.R. Taylor) (Oxford: Clarendon, 1957).

Grimm, Jacob. *Teutonic Mythology* (4 vols; 4th Ed., James S. Stallybrass, Trans.) (New York: Dover, 1966 [Orig. pub. 1883, 1888]).

Guerber, H.A. *Myths of Northern Lands* (New York: American Book Co., 1895).

Hallowell, A.I. *Culture and Experience.* (Philadelphia: University of Pensylvania Press, 1955).

Haugen, Einar. *The Scandinavian Languages* (Cambridge, Mass: Harvard University Press, 1976).

Hope, Murry. 'Practical Rune Magic,' *Fate*, 38: 3, 1985.

James, William. *The Principles of Psychology* (2 vols.) (New York: Dover, 1950 [Orig. Pub. 1890]).

Jones, Gwyn (Trans.). *Egils Saga* (New York: Syracuse University Press, 1960).

Jung, Carl G. 'Synchronizität als ein Prinzip akausaler Zusammenhänge.' In Jung, Carl G. and Pauli, Wolfgang. *Naturklärung und Psyche* (Zürich: C.G. Jung Institut, 1954).

Jung, Carl G. *Synchronicity: An Acausal Connecting Principle* (R.F. Hull, Trans.) (New Jersey: Princeton University Press, 1973).

Jung, Carl G. (Ed.) *Man and his Symbols* (Garden City, NY: Doubleday, 1964).

Klingenberg, Heinz. *Runenschrift-Schriftdenken-Runeninschriften* (Heidelberg: Karl Winter Universitätsverlag, 1973).

Kohl, Johann, G. *Kitchi-Gami: Life Among the Lake Superior Ojibway* (Lascelles Wraxall, Trans.) (St. Paul: University of Minnesota Press, 1985).

Lord, Garman. 'Your Future in the Runes,' *Fate*, 36: 9, 1983.

Lowie, Robert. *Primitive Religion* (New York: Liveright, 1948).

Magnusson, Magnus & Palsson, Hermann (Trans.). *The Vinland Sagas: Graenlendinga Saga and Eirik's Saga* (New York University Press, 1966).

Malinowski, B. *Magic, Science and Religion and Other Essays* (Garden City, New York: Doubleday, 1955).

McCulloch, John A. *The Mythology of All Races* (Vol. 2: Eddic) (Boston: Archaeological Institute of America, 1930).

McDougall, William. *Body and Mind* (Westport, CT: Greenwood Press, 1974 [Orig. pub. 1911]).

Munch, Peter Andreas. *Norse Mythology* (S.B. Hustvedt, Trans.) (Detroit: Singing Tree Press, 1968).

Norbeck, Edward. *Religion in Primitive Society* (New York: Harper & Row, 1961).

Oxenstierna, Eric. *The Norsemen* (Catherine Hutter, Trans.) (Greenwich, CT: New York Graphic Society, 1965).

Page, R.I. *An Introduction to English Runes* (London: Methuen, 1973).

Palsson, Hermann & Edwards, Paul (Trans.). *The Book of Settlements (Landnamabok)* (Winnipeg: University of Manitoba Press, 1972).

Piaget, Jean. *The Child's Conception of the World* (Joan & Andrew Tomlinson, Trans.) (Totowa, NJ: Littlefield, Adams, 1967 [Orig. pub. 1929]).

Schneider, Karl. *Die Germanischen Runenamen: Versuch einer Gesamtdeutung* (Meisenheim am Glan: Anton Hein Verlag, 1956).

Sheldrake, Rupert. *A New Science of Life* (Los Angeles: Tarcher, 1981).

Shetelig, Haakon and Falk, Hjalmar (E.V. Gordon, Trans.). *Scandinavian Archaeology* (New York: Hacker Art Books, 1978).

Stephens, George. *Handbook of the Old Northern Runic Monuments* (London: Williams & Northgate, 1884).

Sturlusson, Snorri (Jean I. Young, Trans.). *The Prose Edda* (Berkeley: University of California Press, 1954).

Tacitus, C. Germania (M. Hutton and E.H. Warmington, Trans.). In *Tacitus in Five Volumes* (Cambridge, Mass.: Harvard University Press, 1914).

Terry, Patricia. *Poems of the Vikings* (Indianapolis: Bobbs-Merrill, 1969).

Thalbitzer, William. *Two Runic Stones, from Greenland and Minnesota* (Washington: Smithsonian Institution, 1951).

Turville-Petre, E.O.G. *Myth and Religion of the North* (New York: Holt, Rinehart & Winston, 1964).

Turville-Petre, G. *The Heroic Age of Scandinavia* (London: Hutchinson, 1951).

Vigfusson, Gudbrand and Powell, F. York (Ed. & Trans.). *Corpus Poeticum Boreale: The Poetry of the Old Northern tongue* (2 vols.) (Oxford: Clarendon Press, 1883).

INDEX